Contents

River landscapes **21**
Profile of rivers
Hydrographs
Fluvial processes
Fluvial landform processes. **22**
Fluvial landforms resulting from erosion
Fluvial landforms resulting from deposition
Fluvial landforms resulting from erosion and deposition
Management strategies for floods. **23**
Management strategies to protect coastlines
Factors affecting flood risk
Case study – flood relief projects
Glacial landscapes **24**
Glacial processes
Economic activities in glaciated upland areas
Land use conflicts
Case study – glacial areas
Glacial landform processes **25**
Glacial landforms resulting from erosion
Glacial landforms resulting from transportation and deposition

HUMAN GEOGRAPHY

Patterns of urban change **26**
Key terms
Case study – urbanisation opportunities and challenges
Case study – urban change in the UK
Urban sustainability and patterns of urban development **27**
Urban sustainability
Measures of development
Case study – urban sustainability
Demographic Transition Model (DMI)
Global development gap and global aid **28**
Strategies to reduce the development gap
Case study – tourism development
Types of aid
Uneven development
Rapid economic development. **29**
Case study – effects of rapid economic development

Economic changes in the UK. . . . .
Causes of economic change in the UK
Moving towards a post-industrial economy
Impacts of industry on the environment
Case study – past and present impacts
The North-South Divide
Economic changes in the UK. **31**
Social and economic changes in rural landscapes
Improvements and new developments
Links between UK and the wider world
Resource management **32**
Resources affecting wellbeing
Global inequalities in supply & consumption of resources
Resource use in the UK
Food supply. **33**
Global patterns of food supply
Factors affecting food supply
Impacts of food supply scarcity
Strategies to increase food supply
Case study – food supply development projects
Food supply and water supply. **34**
Sustainability strategies for the future of food supply
Case study – food and water development projects
Global patterns of water supply
Factors affecting water supply
Water supply **35**
Impacts of water supply scarcity
Strategies to increase water supply
Case study – water development projects
Sustainability strategies for the future of water supply
Case study – sustainable water supply
Energy supply. **36**
Global patterns of energy supply
Factors affecting energy supply
Impacts of energy supply scarcity
Case study – energy supply projects
Energy supply. **37**
Strategies to increase energy supply
Sustainability strategies for the future of energy supply
Case study – sustainable energy supply

Natural and tectonic hazards

Defining natural hazards

- **Natural hazard:** a severe event that can significantly harm individuals, property, and the surrounding environment. Types of natural hazards include:
  - **Geographical hazards:** caused by rocks and tectonic plate movement. Examples include tsunamis, earthquakes, volcanoes, and landslides.
  - **Meteorological hazards:** extreme weather conditions. Examples include: tornadoes, droughts, floods, and heat waves.

Factors affecting hazard risks

- **Location:** people often live in hazardous areas because they have no choice or cannot afford to relocate. Some areas, like areas near volcanoes, have fertile soil rich in minerals (e.g. phosphorus), which is ideal for farming and supports livelihoods.
- **Climate change:** human activities, such as **deforestation** and **industrial processes** (e.g. emitting greenhouse gases), have increased global temperatures. This leads to more frequent and intense **landslides** and **tropical storms**.
- **Urbanisation:** contributes further by increasing greenhouse gas emissions and clearing forests to make space for buildings.
- **Ability to cope and predictability:** this is largely dependent on how wealthy and well-resourced a nation or region is to respond to a natural hazard.
  - **High-income countries (HICs)**, like Japan, have more resources and advanced technology to predict and manage natural disasters. For example: Japan uses earthquake-resistant buildings to absorb shock waves and reduce damage.
  - **Poorer countries (LICs),** like Nepal, lack the money to invest in such infrastructures, making them more vulnerable. As a result, similar disasters cause **greater damage and loss of life** in LICs compared to HICs.
- Some natural hazards are inherently more destructive, especially those occurring near tectonic plate boundaries, where earthquakes and volcanic eruptions are likely.

Plate tectonics theory

All specs except:
OCR A, Edexcel A

The Earth's natural hazards, such as earthquakes and volcanoes, are primarily caused by the movement of tectonic plates. These plates move due to forces generated by processes like ridge push and slab pull. As the plates move, they interact at their boundaries, leading to various natural hazards:

- **Earthquakes** occur when plates grind against each other or suddenly release built-up stress.
- **Volcanoes** form when magma escapes to the surface, often at divergent or convergent plate boundaries.
- **Ridge push:** occurs at **constructive** plate margins.
  - When tectonic plates move apart, magma rises from the mantle to fill the gap.
  - As this magma reaches the surface, it cools and hardens, forming new sections of the plate.
  - The rest of the semi-molten magma cools down, becoming heavier and denser, causing it to sink along the ridge.
- **Slab pull:** occurs at **destructive** plate margins.
  - Due to gravity, the denser plate subducts (i.e. sinks) into the mantle.

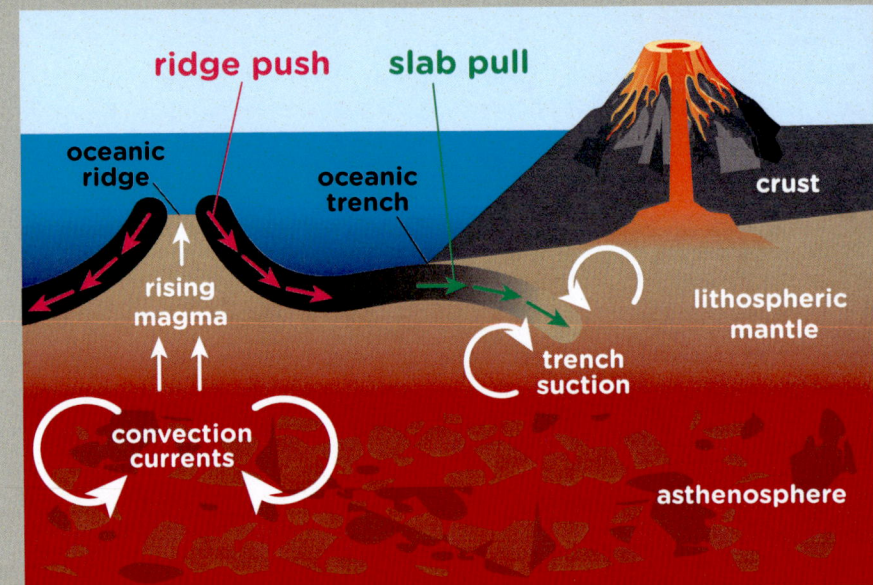

Earth layers and earthquakes

Layers of the Earth

All specs except: OCR A, Edexcel A

- **Crust:** the Earth has two main types of crust:
  - **Oceanic crust:** situated below the ocean and thinner than continental crust. This layer is made of **basalt** which is denser and ideal for subduction.
  - **Continental crust:** found beneath continents and thicker than oceanic crust. This type of crust is made of **granite** which is less dense than basalt.
- **Mantle:** the thickest section of all the earth's layers. (approx. 2,900 km) and made from semi-molten rock (magma).
- **Core:** broken down into two further layers (inner and outer) which are both made from **nickel** and **iron**.
  - The inner core is a solid and the hottest part of the Earth.
  - The outer core is liquid matter.

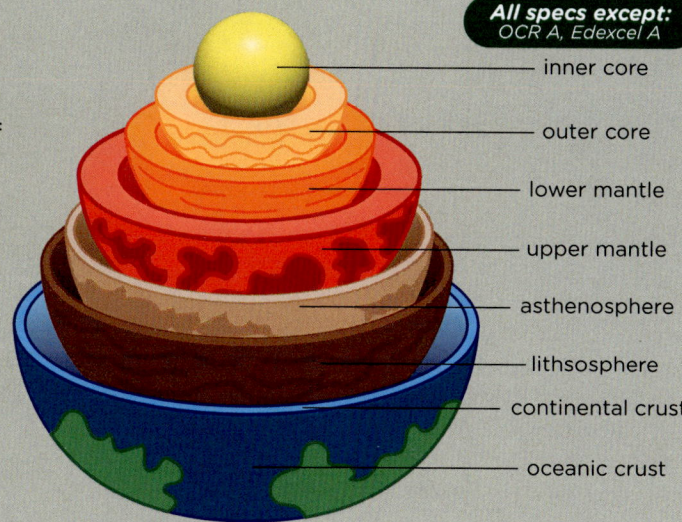

Labels: inner core, outer core, lower mantle, upper mantle, asthenosphere, lithsosphere, continental crust, oceanic crust

Earthquake key terms

All specs except: OCR A, Edexcel A

- **Richter scale:** measures how strong (intense) an earthquake is. The scale goes from 1 to 10 but is logarithmic, meaning that every increase on this scale actually releases x10 the amount of energy (e.g. an earthquake measuring 3 on the Richter scale is barely felt, whereas a 6 is enough to damage buildings near the epicentre).
- **Focus:** is the exact point underground where the earthquake starts. It occurs deep in the Earth's crust where the tectonic plates move.
- **Epicentre:** is a point on the Earth's surface directly above the focus. This is the location where the earthquake is experienced most intensely.

Global distribution of tectonic hazards

All specs except: OCR A, Edexcel A

- Tectonic hazards such as earthquakes and volcanoes mainly occur along plate margins where the different tectonic plates meet.
- Both **destructive** (oceanic plate subducting beneath a continental plate) and **constructive** (plates moving apart) boundaries can produce earthquakes and volcanic eruptions.
- The **Pacific Ring of Fire** is a major zone of tectonic activity, with frequent earthquakes and volcanic eruptions surrounding the Pacific Ocean.
- Earthquakes can also occur away from plate boundaries (**intraplate** earthquakes), but these are less common and usually less intense.
- Tectonic activity is **unevenly distributed** across the globe, with some regions (e.g. parts of Asia, the Americas, and Oceania) experiencing far more hazards than others due to their position along active plate boundaries.

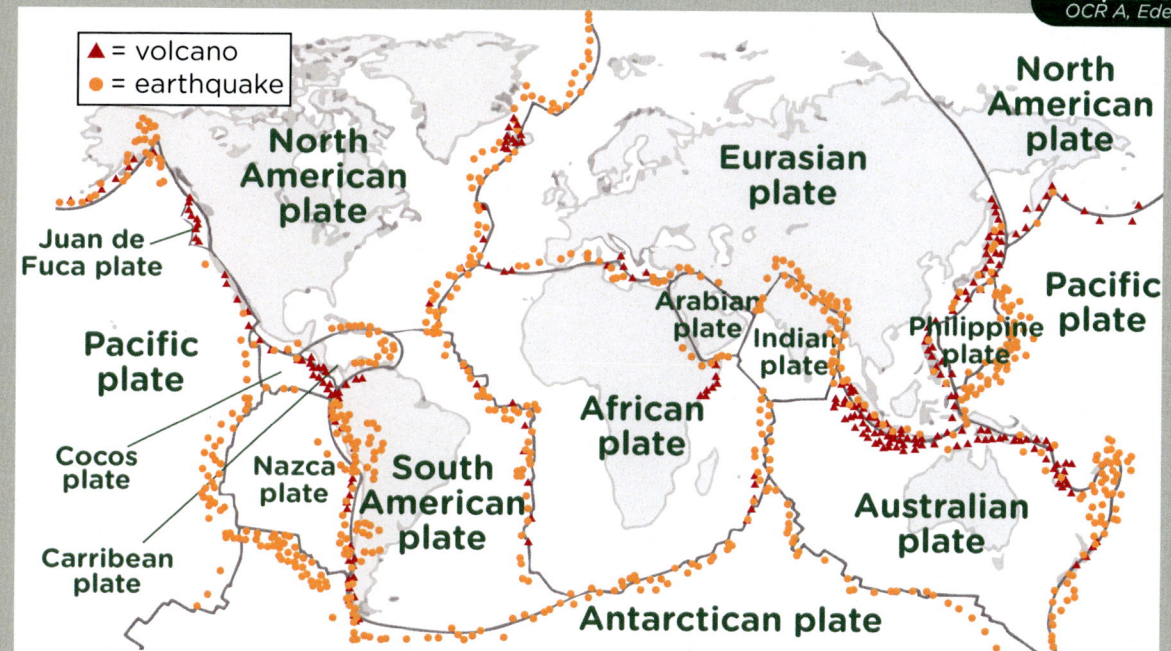

Map legend: ▲ = volcano, ● = earthquake

Plate labels: North American plate, Eurasian plate, Pacific plate, Philippine plate, Juan de Fuca plate, Arabian plate, Indian plate, African plate, Australian plate, Pacific plate, Cocos plate, Nazca plate, South American plate, Carribean plate, Antarctican plate

Tectonic plate margins

Destructive margins

- **Destructive margins** or **convergent boundaries** occur when two tectonic plates move towards each other. This can be:
  - **Oceanic plate + oceanic plate** (e.g. Pacific plate and Philippine plate)
    - One oceanic plate subducts beneath another.
    - This creates deep ocean trenches and island arcs (chains of volcanic islands) as well as earthquakes and volcanic eruptions.
  - **Oceanic plate + continental plate** (e.g. Nazca plate and South American plate)
    - This happens when the oceanic plate is denser than the continental plate and subducts beneath it.
    - As the oceanic plate subducts, it melts due to heat/pressure in the mantle.
    - Magma can rise through cracks, forming volcanoes and fold mountains.
  - **Continental plate + continental plate** (e.g. Indian plate and Eurasian plate)
    - Neither plate is subducted. Instead they crumple and fold, creating fold mountains and powerful earthquakes.
    - No volcanoes can form as there is no subduction/magma.

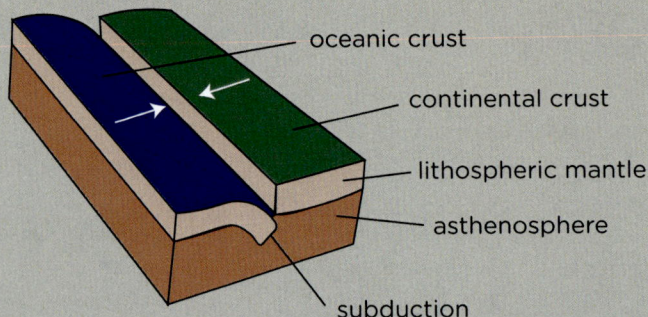

oceanic crust
continental crust
lithospheric mantle
asthenosphere
subduction

Constructive margins

- **Constructive margins** or **divergent boundaries** occur when two tectonic plates move apart. This can be:
  - **Oceanic plate + oceanic plate** (e.g. North American plate and Eurasian plate)
    - As plates move apart, magma rises from the mantle to fill the gap.
    - Magma cools and solidifies to form new oceanic crust, creating ocean ridges, underwater volcanoes, and volcanic islands (e.g. Iceland).
    - Earthquakes may occur from tension as the crust fractures.
  - **Continental plate + continental plate** (less common) where a rift may form as the crust stretches and thins (e.g. East African Rift Valley).

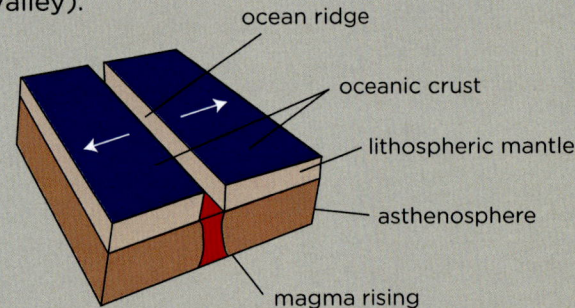

ocean ridge
oceanic crust
lithospheric mantle
asthenosphere
magma rising

Conservative margins

- **Conservative margins** or **transform boundaries** occur when two tectonic plates slide past each other in different directions, or the same direction at different speeds.
  - These cause earthquakes but not volcanoes (e.g. the Pacific and North American plates, creating the San Andreas Fault in California).
  - Pressure builds up over many years until the plates slip past each other, triggering destructive, devastating earthquakes.

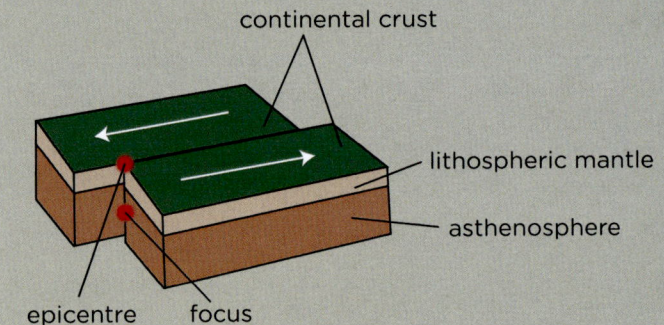

continental crust
lithospheric mantle
asthenosphere
epicentre   focus

Key features of plate margins

Destructive margins	Constructive margins	Conservative margins
Crust is destroyed in subduction zones	New crust is created from magma	No crust created or destroyed
Severe earthquakes	Shallow earthquakes	Powerful earthquakes
Explosive volcanoes with silica-rich magma	Volcanoes with basaltic lava (runny, less explosive)	No volcanic activity as no magma rises
Creates fold mountains and trenches	Creates mid-ocean ridges	Creates fault lines

Effects of tectonic hazards

All specs except:
OCR A, Edexcel A

Primary effects	Secondary effects
• **People injured or killed:** falling debris and collapsing buildings can injure or kill people. Others may be trapped under rubble requiring rescue and medical attention. • **Property damage:** homes, offices, and other buildings can collapse, leaving people homeless or businesses destroyed. • **Transport links damaged:** roads, railways, and ports can be destroyed, making it challenging to get aid to the affected areas. • **Pipes and power lines broken:** water pipes can burst, cutting off water supplies. Electricity cables can snap, causing power cuts.	• **Fires from broken gas pipes:** gas leaks can cause fires which destroy more buildings and put lives at risk. • **Lack of fresh water:** can lead to diseases like cholera if people drink dirty water. • **Blocked transport links:** roads and railways can be blocked by rubble, inhibiting emergency services from helping people. • **Businesses lose money:** shops and factories may have to close due to damage. Governments and people spend more money on repairing buildings instead of growing the economy and improving infrastructure.

Responses to a tectonic hazard

All specs except:
OCR A, Edexcel A

Immediate responses (within 48 hours)	Long-term responses (after 48 hours)
• **Issue warnings:** authorities warn people about aftershocks or further danger to help keep people safe. • **Rescue teams search for survivors:** emergency teams search for people trapped under rubble, using special equipment and dogs to rescue survivors. • **Treat the injured:** doctors and paramedics treat the wounded. Temporary hospitals may be set up if local ones are damaged.	• **Improve building regulations:** use materials and design buildings that can withstand earthquakes. • **Restore utilities:** fix broken water pipes, electricity cables, and gas lines to restore normalcy. • **Resettle locals elsewhere:** move people to safer areas if their homes are destroyed or unsafe, reducing the risk of potential harm. • **Install monitoring technology:** set up equipment to detect earthquakes early, alerting people to prepare.

Case study – responding to earthquakes

All specs except:
OCR A, Edexcel A

	Nepal earthquake (2015)	New Zealand earthquake (2011)
Key details	• Date: 25 April, 2015 • Magnitude: 7.8 • Depth: 15 km • Location: Near Kathmandu, Nepal	• Date: February 22, 2011 • Magnitude: 6.3 • Depth: 5 km (very shallow) • Location: Christchurch, South Island, New Zealand
Primary effects	• Over 8,000 people were killed, and thousands were injured. • Roads and buildings in Kathmandu, the capital of Nepal, were heavily damaged.	• 185 people were killed. • Around 6,000 to 7,000 people were injured. • Buildings were damaged. • Thousands of people were displaced due to damaged or destroyed homes
Secondary effects	• Avalanches and landslides triggered by the earthquake killed 19 people on Mount Everest. • Tourism, a major source of income for Nepal, declined significantly after the disaster.	• The total cost of rebuilding and recovery was estimated in the billions, putting a significant strain on the economy. • Christchurch's tourism industry suffered as visitors avoided the area.
Immediate responses	• The United Nations provided emergency aid, including medical supplies, to help treat the injured. • Rescuers saved people from dangerous situations and transported them to hospitals for treatment.	• 800 farmers, known as the 'Farmy Army,' were mobilised to assist in rescue operations and help people in dangerous areas.
Long-term responses	• 7,000 schools rebuilt to restore essential services. • Damaged sewage and water systems were repaired to improve sanitation.	• £28 billion was invested to rebuild homes, buildings, and infrastructure damaged by the earthquake.

Why people live in tectonic hazard zones

All specs except:
OCR A, Edexcel A

Although these areas are deemed dangerous, people may choose to stay because of economic and/or social reasons.

Economic reasons	Social reasons
• **Fertile soil for farming:** volcanic soil is rich in nutrients, which aids with crop growth. This occurs because volcanic rock breaks down and releases important minerals like potassium and phosphorus. • **Tourism/job opportunities:** volcanic and tectonic landscapes often attract tourists, enabling locals to earn a living within the tourism industry. Activities like hiking, hot springs, and sightseeing bring revenue to the area. • **Cheap geothermal power:** in places like Iceland, geothermal heat produces cheap and clean energy, providing electricity and heating for homes and businesses. • **Mining opportunities:** valuable materials like sulphur can be mined near volcanoes, providing jobs and income for local people. • **Lack of resources required to move:** relocating can be expensive, especially for low-income families. Housing, transport, and starting a new life elsewhere may be financially infeasible, so people remain despite the risks	• **Difficulties relocating:** some areas at risk, like Naples in Italy, have grown into huge cities. Moving such large populations would be expensive and difficult. • **Family and community ties:** people often have strong social connections in the area, including family, friends, and community support networks, as well as generations of family history and legacy, making it emotionally difficult to consider leaving. • **Cultural or religious significance:** some tectonic regions hold deep cultural or religious importance (e.g. Mount Fuji in Japan). • **Overconfidence in technology and emergency services:** in developed countries, people often believe that building regulations, warning systems, and emergency response plans will protect them. This sense of security can reduce the perceived risk of living in a hazardous area. • **Lack of education or risk awareness:** in some cases, residents may not fully understand the risks due to limited education or access to information. Without awareness of the potential dangers, they are less likely to relocate.

Reducing risks of tectonic hazards

All specs except:
OCR A, Edexcel A

- **Monitoring:** scientists use technology to track signs of tectonic activity, allowing people to prepare. Examples include:
  - **Seismometers:** measure earth movements to detect earthquakes.
  - **Gas monitoring:** volcanoes release gases like sulphur dioxide before erupting.
  - **Earthquake patterns:** small earthquakes can signal a volcanic eruption.
- **Prediction:** by observing and analysing data from monitoring, scientists can predict when and where a tectonic event might happen. For example, if a volcano shows signs of activity, people can evacuate before it erupts.
  - **Volcanic prediction:** changes in gas emissions, ground deformation, and temperature increases can indicate an imminent eruption
  - **Earthquake forecasting:** while exact prediction is not currently possible, areas with frequent minor tremors or strain build-up along fault lines can be identified as high-risk zones.
  - **Historical data analysis:** patterns from past tectonic events help identify vulnerable regions and anticipate future hazards.
  - **Warning systems:** data from prediction models can trigger alerts, enabling early warning systems to inform the public and emergency services.
- **Protection:** steps are taken to reduce damage to buildings and infrastructure. This may include:
  - **Reinforced buildings:** designed to absorb earthquake movement and prevent collapse.
  - **Automatic shutdowns:** gas and electricity systems turn off during earthquakes to prevent fires.
  - **Lava diversion:** trenches and barriers are built to stop lava from reaching towns.
- **Planning:** governments and communities prepare for tectonic hazards in advance. Planning ensures people are aware on what to do and where to go, reducing panic and saving lives. For example:
  - **Avoid building in risky areas:** do not build homes near fault lines or active volcanoes.
  - **Training and drills:** emergency services and the public practise drills in the event of a tectonic hazard.
  - **Evacuation routes:** clear routes are planned to help people escape quickly.
  - **Emergency supplies:** stockpiles of food, water, and medical supplies are prepared.

General atmospheric circulation model: pressure belts and surface winds

All specs except: CIE

Key features of atmospheric circulation:
- **Hadley cell:** the cycle of warm air rising at the equator and cool air sinking at about 30° latitude. This creates trade winds and subtropical high pressure.
- **Ferrel cell:** the middle latitudes (between 30° and 60°) where warm air moves poleward, and cool air moves toward the equator. This creates westerly winds and is associated with low pressure around 60°.
- **Polar cell**: in the polar regions, cold air sinks and moves toward the equator, creating easterly winds and high pressure near the poles.

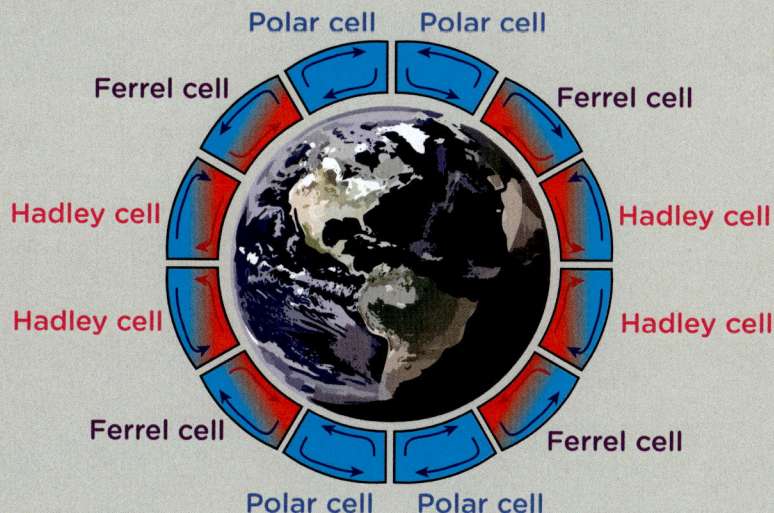

Coriolis effect

All specs except: CIE

The direction of a tropical storm spin is caused by the **Coriolis effect** which is a result of the Earth's rotation. This effect influences the movement of air and triggers storms to spin in opposite directions depending on the hemisphere.
- In the **northern hemisphere,** tropical storms spin **anticlockwise** because the Coriolis effect deflects moving air to the **right** in that hemisphere.
- In the **southern hemisphere,** tropical storms spin **clockwise** because the Coriolis effect deflects moving air to the **left** in that hemisphere.

Impacts of weather hazards in the UK

All specs except: CIE, Pearson IGCSE

- **Drought:** crops fail, food prices rise, hosepipe bans (e.g. 2012 UK Drought).
- **Freezing temperatures:** hypothermia, car accidents, pressure on the NHS (e.g. The Big Freeze in 2010).
- **Heavy rainfall:** flooding causes landslides, destroying crops and homes (e.g. Cumbria floods in 2009).
- **Thunderstorms:** lightning strikes damage buildings and infrastructure (e.g. North Yorkshire in 2005).
- **Heatwaves:** droughts cause crops to fail, and vulnerable people suffer from heatstroke (e.g. June heatwave in 2017).

Case study – extreme weather hazards

All specs except: CIE, Pearson IGCSE

The Big Freeze (2010)	
Key details	• Date: December 2010 • Location: United Kingdom and Ireland • North-east winds brought cold Arctic air and heavy snow. • Temperatures dropped below 0°C, and snow reached a depth of 50 cm in some areas.
Social impacts	• **School closures:** several schools closed, causing children to miss education and requiring parents to make alternate arrangements for childcare, potentially missing work. • **Water shortages:** in Northern Ireland, 40,000 homes were left without water due to frozen pipes. • **Isolation and accidents:** icy roads caused traffic accidents, and some communities isolated.
Economic impacts	• **Car accidents:** on 20 December, the AA reported its busiest day ever due to road accidents. • **Disrupted sales and transport:** shops witnessed a drop in sales, and transportation was severely disrupted. • **Water shortages:** 40,000 homes were left without water, affecting daily life.
Environmental impact	• **Crop damage:** snow and freezing temperatures damaged crops. • **Energy use:** gas and electricity bills were doubled the usual amount for December.
Management strategies to reduce risks	• **Weather warnings:** advance warnings help people prepare for extreme weather. • **Insulated walls:** insulating cavity walls prevent pipes from freezing and provide warmth. • **Indoor farming:** protecting crops indoors can reduce the impact of future extreme weather events on crops.

Tropical storm hazards

Formation of tropical storms

All specs except: CIE

Tropical storms (hurricanes, cyclones, and typhoons) occur in **low latitudes**, typically between **5° and 30° north and south of the equator**, within the **Tropics of Cancer and Capricorn**.

The key conditions for formation are **ocean temperatures** (must be above **27°C** to provide the energy required for storm development) and **location** (typically form over oceans in tropical regions).

The 3 types of tropical storms are:

- **Hurricanes:**
  - Form in the Atlantic Ocean and the eastern Pacific Ocean
  - Common in the Northern Hemisphere.
- **Cyclones:**
  - Form in the South Pacific Ocean or the Indian Ocean
  - Common in the Southern Hemisphere
- **Typhoons:**
  - Forms in the Northwest Pacific Ocean
  - Common in the Western Pacific region

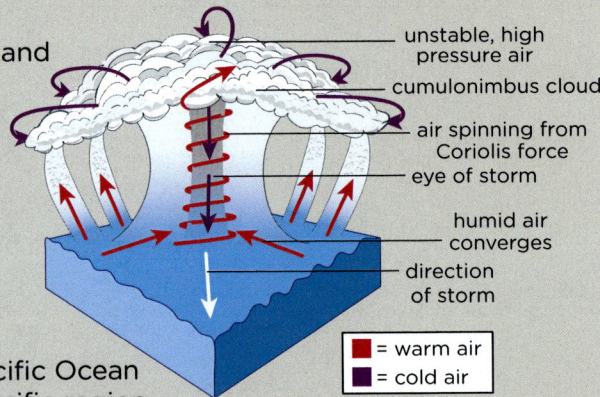

Labels: unstable, high pressure air; cumulonimbus cloud; air spinning from Coriolis force; eye of storm; humid air converges; direction of storm

■ = warm air
■ = cold air

The sequence of tropical storm formation and development is:

1. **Warm ocean water heats the air:** the sun heats the tropical seas, causing water to evaporate. Warm, moist air rises rapidly, creating **low pressure**.
2. **Air rises and spins:** as the air rises, it begins to spin due to the **Coriolis effect**. This creates a rotating system with a calm, clear **eye** at the centre.
3. **Cloud formation and rainfall:** the rising air cools and condenses, forming large cumulonimbus clouds. This leads to **heavy rainfall** and releases **heat**, which further powers the storm.
4. **Storm intensifies:** the continuous cycle of rising air, condensation, and heat release strengthens the storm. Strong winds develop as air rushes toward the low-pressure centre.
5. **Landfall weakens the storm:** when the storm reaches land, it loses its energy source (warm ocean water). The storm weakens and eventually dissipates.

Distribution of tropical storms

All specs except: CIE

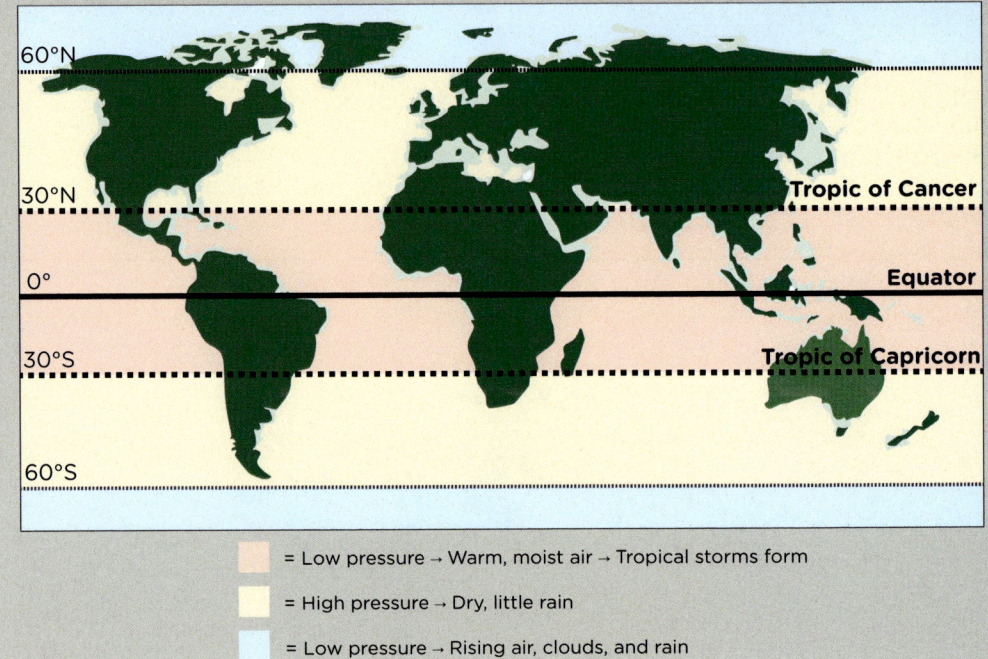

Labels: 60°N; 30°N; 0°; 30°S; 60°S; Tropic of Cancer; Equator; Tropic of Capricorn

■ = Low pressure → Warm, moist air → Tropical storms form

■ = High pressure → Dry, little rain

■ = Low pressure → Rising air, clouds, and rain

Effect of climate change on tropical storm distribution, frequency, and intensity

All specs except: CIE

- **Distribution:** rising sea temperatures due to climate change may expand in areas where tropical storms can form. This can lead to frequent storms in the South Atlantic, where tropical storms are rare, and more storms forming in the subtropics (areas further from the equator) as warmer seas provide the necessary conditions for storm development.
- **Frequency:** the overall frequency of tropical storms is expected to remain or decrease. However, the types of storms may change: Category 1–3 storms (weaker storms) are expected to decrease, whereas Category 4 and 5 storms (the most intense storms) are expected to increase due to warmer seas providing more energy, fuelling stronger storms.
- **Intensity:** the intensity of tropical storms is likely to increase as sea surface temperatures rise. Warmer oceans provide energy for storms, leading to stronger winds, heavier rainfall, and more destructive storms overall.

Reducing risks of tropical storms

All specs except: CIE

- **Prediction:**
  - **Satellite data:** tracks early signs of cyclonic activity over warm ocean waters to identify potential storm formation days in advance.
  - **Supercomputers and weather models:** simulate storm paths and strength, combining historical data with current atmospheric conditions.
  - **Real-time data collection:** for example, NASA uses two Global Hawk drones to monitor weather across the Atlantic.
  - **Early warning systems:** alert people to evacuate safely, reducing casualties and allowing for time to prepare
- **Monitoring:**
  - **Real-time satellites:** provide continuous visual and infrared imagery. This can detect storm movement, eye formation, cloud structure, and rainfall patterns once storms have formed.
  - **Radar systems:** detect storm position and rainfall intensity as storms approach land. For example, ground-based Doppler radar helps local agencies track storms hour-by-hour.
  - **Weather buoys and ocean sensors:** collect sea-level pressure and temperature data, providing crucial information on storm surges and cyclone development.
- **Planning:**
  - **Land use zoning:** governments restrict buildings from being constructed in high-risk areas (e.g. low-lying coastal zones).
  - **Evacuation routes:** clear evacuation routes to shelters are signposted and maintained for a safe escape during storms.
  - **Community preparedness:** Red Cross educates people on the best ways to respond to tropical storms to prevent injury and loss of life.
  - **Insurance and disaster funding schemes:** helps communities recover financially after storm damage and receive aid to access food, water, medicine, and other essentials
- **Protection:**
  - **Storm-resistant building design:** houses built on stilts to allow floodwater to pass underneath.
  - **High sea walls and storm barriers:** protect coastal areas from storm surges.
  - **Levees and embankments:** reduce the risk of flooding.
  - **Mangrove and wetland conservation:** natural barriers absorb wave energy and reduce risks of flooding from storms and tsunamis.

Case study – tropical storms

All specs except: CIE

Typhoon Haiyan (2013)	
Key details	• Date: 2 November 2013 • Origin: Western Pacific Ocean • Moved over the Philippines at 313 km/hr
Primary effects	• **Deaths:** 6,300 lives were lost. • **Food shortages:** rice crops and coconut plantations were destroyed, leading to a lack of food. • **Homes destroyed:** 1.4 million homes and properties were damaged, leaving many people homeless.
Secondary effects	• **Landslides and blocked roads:** heavy rainfall caused landslides, blocking roads, and delaying aid. • **Homelessness and job loss:** millions of people lost their homes and jobs, adding pressure on household incomes. • **Illnesses from dirty water:** The lack of clean water led to the spread of diseases such as cholera. • **Widespread societal impact:** 14 million people were affected by the typhoon, including those who lost loved ones, homes, or livelihoods.
Immediate responses	• **International aid:** shelter kits were delivered to the Philippines by the UK and Canada. The USA and Japan sent water and essential household items. • **Evacuation centres:** approximately 1,200 evacuation centres were set up or displaced people. • **Field hospitals:** built to treat the injured. • **Temporary shelters:** temporary shelters were provided for people who were displaced or homeless.
Long-term responses	• **Cyclone shelters:** cyclone shelters were constructed to protect people from future storms. • **Restoration of livelihoods:** rice farming and fishing industries were swiftly restored to support the economy and jobs. • **International aid:** the UN and other countries donated financial aid, medical support, and resources to help with long-term recovery.

Causes of climate change

- **Natural factors:**
  - **Orbital changes:** the Earth's orbit is **elliptical**, and its axis is tilted, which changes the amount of the Sun's energy reaching the Earth's surface.
  - **Volcanic activity:** volcanic eruptions release substantial amounts of **sulphur dioxide**, which blocks sunlight and temporarily reduces global temperatures.
  - **Solar output:** the Sun's energy output changes in an **11-year cycle**. Increased sunspots lead to higher global temperatures.
- **Human factors:**
  - **Burning fossil fuels:** burning coal, oil, and gas releases CO_2, accounting for **50% of greenhouse gas emissions**.
  - **Agriculture:** farming livestock and growing crops like rice produce methane, contributing to 20% of greenhouse gas emissions.
  - **Deforestation:** felling trees for agriculture or logging increases CO_2 levels because there are limited trees to absorb CO_2 through photosynthesis.
  - **Industrial processes:** manufacturing and chemical production release greenhouse gases like CO_2, methane, and nitrous oxide.

Effects of climate change

- **Effects on people:**
  - **Health impacts:** increased risk of diseases, such as malaria, due to warmer climates, and higher rates of skin cancer and heat stroke caused by rising temperatures.
  - **Food production:** crop yields have decreased by up to 12% in South America, leading to food shortages. Although yields have increased in Northern Europe, irrigation is required to support farming and is expensive to maintain.
  - **Economic opportunities:** less ice in the Arctic Ocean allows for increased shipping routes and easier extraction of oil and gas reserves.
- **Effects on the environment:**
  - **Droughts:** increased drought in the Mediterranean region will lead to more food shortages.
  - **Coral bleaching:** rising sea temperatures cause coral bleaching. By 2100, it is expected that 98% of coral reefs will be bleached.
  - **Forests:** are increasingly affected by pests, diseases, and forest fires, damaging ecosystems and reducing biodiversity.

Evidence for climate change

Evidence shows that the climate has changed from the **Quaternary Period** (2.6 million years ago) to the present day:

- **Met office records:** reliable temperature records have been kept since 1914.
- **Tree rings**: grow wider in warm, wet conditions and thinner in cold, dry conditions. These provide reliable data for the past 10,000 years.
- **Pollen analysis:** different pollen species require specific climatic conditions, helping scientists understand past climates.
- **Temperature records:** historical records, such as harvest dates and weather reports, provide evidence of past climate conditions.
- **Ice cores:** drilled from ice sheets, containing air bubbles that depict past levels of greenhouse gases.
- **Sediment cores:** organisms that remain in ocean beds provide data for up to 5 million years ago.

Managing climate change

Mitigation (reducing the causes of climate change)	Adaptation (responding to the effects of climate change)
- **Alternative energy production:** using renewable energy sources (e.g. solar, wind, hydroelectric) reduces CO_2 and greenhouse gas emissions. - **Carbon capture and storage (CCS):** captures up to 90% of CO_2 from emission sources (e.g. power plants). CO_2 is safely stored underground beneath impermeable rock. - **Planting trees:** trees absorb CO_2 during photosynthesis, helping to reduce CO_2 levels. Forests can absorb up to 28% of global CO_2 emissions. - **International agreements:** countries work together to reduce emissions. For example, the 2015 Paris Climate Agreement, signed by 195 countries, aims to limit global warming to 1.5°C.	- **Changes in agricultural systems:** farmers adapt to changing rainfall patterns, temperatures, and pests/diseases. Strategies include irrigation systems and growing drought-resistant crops. - **Managing water supply:** installing water-efficient devices to reduce water usage, and increasing water supply through desalination plants and improved irrigation systems. - **Reducing risks from rising sea levels:** building flood defences, such as the Thames Flood Barrier. Raising buildings on stilts or higher ground also helps avoid flooding.

SNAPREVISE

Components of ecosystems

Changing one component in an ecosystem can disrupt the balance and affect all other components. For example, reducing the number of plants can affect the species that feed on it, which leads to that species decline.

- **Producers:** organisms (e.g. plants) that produce their own food through photosynthesis.
- **Consumers:** organisms that gain energy by consuming other organisms. (Biotic factor)
- **Decomposers:** fungi and bacteria that break down dead organic matter, which allow the recycling of nutrients.
- **Food chains:** show how energy flows through an ecosystem, from producers → consumers → decomposers.
- **Food webs:** demonstrate how multiple food chains are interconnected within an ecosystem.
- **Nutrient cycle:** explains how nutrients (e.g. nitrogen, carbon) are recycled between living organisms and the environment.

Distribution and characteristics of large-scale ecosystems

- **Biomes** are regions with specific climate conditions (e.g. based on temperature or rainfall). Examples of biomes include:
  - **Tropical rainforests:** found near the equator (e.g. Amazon, Congo) where it is hot and humid.
  - **Deserts:** found around 30° north and south of the equator (e.g. Sahara) where it is hot and dry.
  - **Tundra:** found near the poles (e.g. Arctic) where it is cold and dry.
- Each biome has unique **climates, vegetation, and wildlife** adapted to its environment.
  - Rainforests have dense vegetation, high biodiversity, and are warm and wet all year.
  - Deserts have sparse vegetation, extreme temperatures, and low rainfall.
  - Tundra has low-growing plants, cold temperatures, and permafrost.

Case study

Example of a small-scale ecosystem: a freshwater pond in Wiltshire
- **Algae** (biotic factor) grows on the pond's surface due to excess nutrients, often from duck food.
- **Plants** use sunlight for photosynthesis, and the roots absorb water and mineral ions from the soil.
- **Insects** feed on plants, while some organisms consume dead matter in areas with low oxygen (anoxic conditions).

Upland/lowland areas in the UK

All specs except: CIE, Pearson IGCSE

Upland	Lowland
- **Scottish Highlands:** rugged mountains made from hard-resistant rock like granite. This region is home to the highest mountain in the UK, Ben Nevis (1,345m). - **Dartmoor:** moorland in south-west UK made from granite (igneous rock). - **The Lake District:** a mountainous region in north-west England, with the greatest number of peaks ranging between 400-800 metre in height. However, it also includes higher peaks, such as Scafell Pike (978m), the highest mountain in England.	- **East Anglia:** a lowland area made from weak sedimentary rocks such as clay, sand, and chalk. It is close to sea level, with flat terrain and fertile soils, ideal for farming. - **Southern England:** features lowland valleys and rolling hills, often found between areas of chalk (e.g. the South Downs) and limestone. These areas are known for their gentle relief and suitability for mixed farming.

River systems in the UK

All specs except: CIE, Pearson IGCSE

- **River Severn:** the longest river in the UK, stretching 354 km. Its source is in the Cambrian Mountains in Wales, at Plynlimon. The river flows through Wales and England, passing through towns before emptying into the Bristol Channel.
- **River Thames:** the second-longest river in the UK, at 346 km in length. It flows entirely through England, starting in the Cotswolds (at Thames Head) and passes through major cities such as Oxford, Reading, and London, before reaching the North Sea. River Thames is significant for its historical, cultural, and economic importance.

SNAPREVISE

Physical characteristics of tropical rainforests
All specs except: *Pearson IGCSE*

The rainforest ecosystem is **interdependent** as it relies on climate, water, soil, plants, animals, and people interacting. For example, the consistent climate supports dense vegetation, providing animal habitats, while decomposing plant matter enriches the soil. However, human activities like deforestation can disrupt this balance.

- **Climate:**
  - Consistently extremely wet, with over 2,000 mm of rainfall per year.
  - Hot and humid, with an average temperature of 28°C.
- **Soil:**
  - Mostly infertile, with a thin layer of fertile soil on the surface where decomposed leaves provide nutrients.
  - Red due to high iron content.
  - Heavy rainfall removes nutrients from the soil, making it nutrient poor.
- **Plants and animals:**
  - Many species are adapted to rainforest conditions (e.g. trees and plants have shallow roots to absorb nutrients from the thin fertile topsoil).
  - Plants have drip tips or pointed leaves that allow water to move off quickly, preventing water from collecting on the leaves which could cause damage to the plant.
  - Plants that grow on the branches of trees in the canopy absorb nutrients and moisture from the air and rain, rather than relying on soil. This adaptation helps them survive high in the canopy where sunlight is abundant but with limited soil access.
  - Animal species native to rainforests also adapt to their environments. For example, spider monkeys have long, strong limbs, which aids them climb and swing between trees in the canopy to find food and avoid predators. Likewise, sloths use camouflage (allowing algae to grow on their fur, giving them a greenish tint) and move very slowly to avoid detection by predators.

Value of tropical rainforests

- For people, rainforests provide resources (e.g. food, medicine, raw materials) and support livelihoods through farming, logging, and tourism.
- For the environment, rainforests function as a carbon sink by absorbing CO_2 and help regulate the Earth's climate. They also maintain biodiversity by providing habitats for many species and prevent soil erosion and regulate the water cycle, reducing the risk of flooding and drought.

Biodiversity issues in tropical rainforests
All specs except: *Pearson IGCSE*

- **Deforestation:** often caused by logging, agriculture (e.g. palm oil and cattle farming), and urban development, destroys vast areas of forest and the habitats within them.
- **Pollution:** from mining, agriculture (e.g. pesticides and fertilisers), and industrial waste can poison water sources and soil, harming biodiversity.
- **Overfishing and hunting:** (including illegal poaching) reduce animal populations and threaten species with extinction, particularly in areas with river systems like the Amazon.
- **Climate change:** alters temperature and rainfall patterns, which can shift or shrink the suitable habitats for many rainforest species.
- **Habitat fragmentation:** (breaking up forests into smaller, isolated patches) makes it harder for species to find food, mates, or migrate, and increases vulnerability to predators and disease.
- **Food webs weakened:** the removal of key species can have cascading effects on other organisms that depend on them, reducing biodiversity.

Deforestation of tropical rainforests
All specs except: *Pearson IGCSE*

Deforestation is the removal of forests, and its rates have changed over time. Globally, around 10 million hectares of forest are lost each year, but the rate has slowed since the 1990s. However, tropical regions, like the Amazon and Congo Basin, still face elevated levels of deforestation.

- **Causes:** farming (e.g. cattle ranching, palm oil, and soy production) is the biggest cause, responsible for over 90% of tropical deforestation. Other causes include logging, mining, building roads, and forest fires.
- **Regional trends:**
  - **Brazil and Colombia:** once had the highest deforestation rates globally. In 2022, Brazilian forest loss accounted for 43% of global deforestation.
  - **Bolivia, Laos, and Nicaragua:** deforestation is increasing due to farming, fires, and mining.
  - **Congo Basin (e.g. DRC):** high deforestation continues due to farming, charcoal production, and mining.
- **Impacts:** loss of biodiversity (plants and animals), contribution to climate change (less carbon dioxide absorbed by trees), and soil erosion and loss of nutrients.
- **Positive changes:** some countries, like Indonesia, have reduced deforestation through appropriate policies. Reforestation (planting trees) is helping, but it cannot fully replace natural forests.

Management of tropical rainforests

All specs except:
Pearson IGCSE

Tropical rainforests need to be managed to be sustainable. Strategies for sustainable management include:

- **Selective logging and replanting:**
  - Selective logging means only certain trees (e.g. mature trees or specific species) felled. This helps maintain biodiversity and reduces damage to the ecosystem.
  - Felled trees are also replaced with new ones via replanting to ensure the forest regenerates and continues to provide resources sustainably.
- **Conservation and education:**
  - Conservation involves protecting areas of rainforest through National Parks or wildlife reserves where human activities like logging and farming are restricted by law. This helps preserve biodiversity and ecosystems.
  - Teaching local communities and the wider public about the importance of rainforests and how to reduce damage. Education can promote sustainable practices and raise awareness of the global benefits of rainforests.
- **Ecotourism:**
  - Encourages sustainable tourism that benefits local communities and protects the rainforest.
  - Provides jobs for locals (e.g. as guides or in hospitality) and offers higher salaries than industries like mining or logging.
  - Teaches locals and visitors how to protect the rainforest while generating income without causing harm.
- **International agreements on tropical hardwoods:**
  - Agreements like the **Forest Stewardship Council (FSC)** promotes sustainable use of tropical hardwoods.
  - These agreements ensure that wood products are sourced responsibly, reducing illegal logging and deforestation.
- **Debt reduction (debt-for-nature swaps):**
  - Some countries with rainforests have large debts to other nations. In a debt-for-nature swap, part of the debt is forgiven in exchange for protecting the rainforest. This helps reduce deforestation while supporting conservation efforts.

Case study – deforestation of rainforests

	Deforestation in Malaysia
Causes	• **Subsistence farming:** land is cleared by local people to grow food for their families. Large-scale plantations, especially for palm oil, are established to export products for profit. • **Logging:** Malaysia is one of the largest exporters of tropical wood. Trees are felled for timber to sell and export. • **Road building:** roads are constructed to provide access for miners, farmers, and logging companies to remote areas of the rainforest. • **Population growth:** forests are cleared to create settlements and farmland to support Malaysia's growing population and economy. • **Mining and energy:** tin mining, oil and gas drilling occur in the rainforest to generate income and improve energy security. • **Tourism development:** forests are sometimes cleared for infrastructure such as hotels, resorts, and transportation to accommodate the growth of tourism industries, particularly adventure tourism in more remote locations like rainforests.
Impacts	• **Economic development:** although jobs in industries like logging, mining, and farming boost Malaysia's economy, local people are often exploited by companies, working in dangerous conditions for low income and ultimately harming the economy and population in the long term. • **Soil erosion:** without tree roots to bind the soil, heavy tropical rain washes soil and nutrients away, leading to soil erosion and a higher risk of flooding. • **Contribution to climate change:** trees store carbon dioxide (CO_2). When they are cut down or burned, CO_2 is released, contributing to global warming. • **Loss of biodiversity:** habitat destruction endangers ecosystems and threatens endangered species like orangutans and Malayan tigers. • **Disruption to indigenous communities:** deforestation displaces people and compromises their way of life.

Physical characteristics of hot deserts

Only: AQA, OCR A

- **Climate:**
  - Hot deserts have an arid (extremely dry) climate with very low precipitation, typically receiving **less than 250mm of rainfall** per year.
  - Rainfall is often unpredictable and can occur in short, intense bursts that may lead to flash flooding, as the dry ground is often unable to absorb water quickly.
  - Temperatures are extreme and show a **high diurnal range** (difference between day and night temperatures).
  - In summer, daytime temperatures can exceed 40°C, while at night, temperatures can drop below 0°C due to the lack of cloud cover, which allows rapid heat loss.
- **Soil**
  - Desert soils are typically **shallow, dry, sandy or stony,** and have very low organic content due to sparse vegetation.
  - They are usually **infertile and nutrient-poor,** lacking the moisture and organic material needed to support dense plant growth.
  - Evaporation often leaves behind salts on the soil surface, forming a hard, crusty layer called **caliche**, which can further hinder water infiltration and plant growth.
  - Some areas may have slightly richer soils around **ephemeral streams** or **oases**, where moisture and nutrients temporarily accumulate.
- **Location:**
  - Hot deserts are generally found between 15° and 30° north and south of the Equator, along the **Tropic of Cancer** and **Tropic of Capricorn**.
  - These are **subtropical high-pressure zones** where descending dry air from the Hadley Cell prevents cloud formation and rainfall.

Adaptations of plants and animals in hot deserts

Only: AQA, OCR A

- Plants:
  - **Xerophytes:** adapted to dry conditions (e.g. cacti with spines to reduce water loss, deep tap roots to access underground water).
  - **Succulents:** store water in stems or leaves.
  - Waxy coatings reduce water loss.
- Animals:
  - Nocturnal behaviour to avoid heat.
  - Camels store fat in humps and can go without water for extended periods.
  - Kangaroo rats get moisture from seeds and live in burrows to escape heat.

Interdependence in hot deserts

Only: AQA, OCR A

- **Climate:** hot and dry conditions limit water availability, affecting plants, animals, and human activities.
- **Water:** scarce water sources (e.g. oases) are vital for plants, animals, and people.
- **Soils:** poor, sandy soils support only drought-resistant plants, which in turn provides food and shelter for animals.
- **Plants and animals:** plants like cacti store water, while animals like camels and fennec foxes are adapted to survive with minimal water.
- **People:** nomadic tribes (e.g. Tuareg people) rely on animals for transport and trade, while farming communities depend on irrigation.

Biodiversity issues in hot deserts

Only: AQA, OCR A

- **Habitat destruction:**
  - **Mining:** involves land clearance and soil disturbance. This destroys habitats and pollutes soil and water (e.g. copper mining in the Atacama Desert in Chile).
  - **Farming:** irrigated agriculture leads to vegetation removal and soil degradation.
  - **Tourism:** construction of resorts, roads, and off-road tracks damages soil and plants. This can cause noise, litter, and pollution which disturbs wildlife.
- **Climate change:**
  - **Higher temperatures:** if temperatures exceed tolerance levels of desert species, they may experience heat stress or even death.
  - **Reduced rainfall:** leads to drying up of water sources like ephemeral rivers and oases, increasing drought conditions.
- **Overuse of water resources:**
  - **Groundwater extraction:** aquifers and underground reserves are depleted by human use. This means water tables fall, making it harder for native plants to survive.
  - **Irrigation impacts:** over-irrigation causes salinisation, making soil infertile. As a result, springs and oases may dry up, leading to local habitat collapse.
  - **Urban and tourist water demand:** increases pressure on already limited resources, reducing availability for ecosystems dependent on natural water sources.

Causes of desertification

Areas on the fringe of hot deserts are at risk of desertification.
- **Climate change:** rising temperatures and reduced rainfall are expanding desert areas. Droughts are becoming more frequent, reducing vegetation cover.
- **Population growth:** increased demand for food, water, and fuel leads to overuse of resources.
- **Removal of fuel wood:** trees and shrubs are cut for firewood, leaving soil exposed to erosion.
- **Overgrazing:** livestock eat vegetation faster than it can regrow, exposing soil to wind erosion.
- **Over-cultivation:** intensive farming depletes soil nutrients, making the land infertile.
- **Soil erosion:** wind and water remove the topsoil, reducing the land's ability to support vegetation.

Management of hot deserts

- **Water and soil management:**
  - **Irrigation systems:** efficient irrigation methods, like **drip irrigation**, deliver water directly to plant roots, reducing water waste and soil erosion.
  - **Bunds:** low stone walls or barriers trap water and prevent soil from being washed away, commonly used in the Sahel region.
- **Crop rotation:** alternating crops helps maintain soil fertility and reduces over-cultivation.
- **Shelterbelts:** planting rows of trees (e.g. the **Great Green Wall** in Africa) acts as windbreaks or shelterbelts, reducing wind erosion and stabilizing the soil. This increases food security as more water is available for agriculture.
- **Use of appropriate technology:** using solar energy for cooking can reduce reliance on wood and protect trees, thereby reducing soil erosion.
- **Afforestation and reforestation:** planting trees and shrubs helps stabilise sandy soils, reduce surface temperatures through shading, and increase moisture retention. Trees also provide habitats for wildlife and can restore degraded ecosystems over time.
- **Education and community involvement:** local communities are trained in sustainable land use practices, such as water conservation, organic farming, and soil restoration techniques.

Case study – development in deserts

Sahara Desert	
Development opportunities	• **Mineral extraction:** the Sahara is rich in resources like phosphate (used in fertilizers), iron ore, and uranium. Countries like Morocco are major exporters of phosphates. • **Solar energy:** the Sahara has vast potential for solar power due to its high levels of sunlight. Projects like the Noor Solar Project in Morocco aim to harness this energy. • **Irrigation:** in areas like the Nile Valley, irrigation allows for farming in deserts. Wheat and barley are cultivated in these areas. • **Oases:** natural water sources in the desert (e.g. Siwa Oasis in Egypt) support small-scale farming. • **Tourism:** the Sahara attracts tourists for activities like camel trekking, sandboarding, and exploring unique landscapes (e.g. sand dunes, rock formations). Cultural tourism includes visiting Berber communities and ancient sites.
Challenges for development	• **Extreme temperatures:** daytime temperatures can exceed 50°C, making outdoor work difficult and increasing the cost of infrastructure maintenance (e.g. roads melting). • **Water supply:** water is scarce, and overuse of underground aquifers (e.g. the Nubian Sandstone Aquifer) risks depleting this resource. Desalination plants are expensive and not widely available. • **Inaccessibility:** the Sahara spans 9.2 million km², making transport and communication difficult. Remote areas lack infrastructure, increasing the cost of development.

Physical characteristics of cold environments

Only: AQA, OCR A, OCR B

- **Polar regions:**
  - **Climate:** extremely cold, with temperatures often below -50°C. Low amounts of precipitation (mostly snow), making it a cold desert.
  - **Landscape:** covered in ice sheets and glaciers, with little exposed land. Examples include Antarctica and Greenland.
  - **Vegetation:** almost no vegetation due to the extreme cold. Some mosses and lichens may grow on exposed rocks.
  - **Wildlife:** limited species adapted to the cold, such as polar bears, penguins, and seals.
- **Tundra:**
  - **Climate:** cold, but less extreme than polar regions. Temperatures can rise above freezing in summer, but winters are long and harsh.
  - **Landscape:** permafrost (permanently frozen ground) underlies the soil. In summer, the top layer thaws, creating boggy conditions.
  - **Vegetation:** low-growing plants like mosses, lichens, grasses, and shrubs. No trees due to the short growing season and frozen soil.
  - **Wildlife:** animals like Arctic foxes, caribou, and snowy owls, adapted to survive the cold and limited food supply.

Adaptations to cold environments

Only: AQA, OCR A, OCR B

- **Plants:**
  - **Small leaves:** reduce water loss through transpiration, which is important in cold, dry conditions.
  - **Dark colours:** some plants have dark-coloured leaves to absorb more heat from the sun.
  - **Shallow roots:** because the permafrost prevents deep growth, and the soil is thin and nutrient-poor.
- **Animals:**
  - **Thick fur or feathers:** animals like polar bears, Arctic foxes, and snowy owls have thick fur or feathers to insulate against the cold.
  - **Camouflage:** Arctic animals like polar bears and Arctic hares have white fur to blend in with the snow, helping them avoid predators or hunt prey.
  - **Small extremities:** animals like Arctic foxes and hares have small ears and tails to reduce heat loss.

Interdependence in cold environments

Only: AQA, OCR A, OCR B

- **Climate:** the cold climate limits plant growth and creates permafrost (permanently frozen ground). Low temperatures and short growing seasons mean plants grow slowly and are small, like mosses and lichens. Animals, such as Arctic foxes and caribou, rely on these plants for food, while predators like polar bears depend on other animals for survival.
- **Permafrost:** affects the soil, making it frozen and nutrient-poor, which limits plant growth. In summer, the top layer of permafrost thaws, allowing plants to grow and providing food for animals. If permafrost melts due to climate change, it releases greenhouse gases like methane, which can further warm the climate.
- **Soil:** soils tend to be thin, frozen, and lack nutrients because of the cold climate and slow decomposition of organic matter. Plants that grow in these soils are adapted to survive with minimal nutrients, and animals depend on these plants for food.
- **Plants:** plants like mosses, lichens, and shrubs provide food and shelter for animals. They also help stabilise the soil and prevent erosion, which is important in areas with thawing permafrost.
- **Animals:** animals are adapted to survive the harsh conditions, such as thick fur or fat for insulation. Herbivores like caribou depend on plants for food, while predators like wolves and polar bears rely on herbivores for food. People in cold environments often rely on animals for food, clothing, and transport (e.g. reindeer herding).

Biodiversity issues in cold environments

Only: AQA, OCR A, OCR B

- **Habitat loss:** deforestation, urbanisation, and agriculture destroy natural habitats. Animals and plants lose their homes, leading to population declines and extinction.
- **Climate change:** rising temperatures, changing weather patterns, and melting ice caps all contribute to a changing climate where species struggle to adapt to new conditions. Polar regions are particularly vulnerable to damage from global warming.
- **Pollution:** plastic waste, chemicals, and oil spills pollute land, water, and air. Pollution harms wildlife, damages ecosystems, and disrupts food chains.
- **Overexploitation:** for example, overfishing, hunting, and logging for resources. Species are pushed to the brink of extinction, and ecosystems become unbalanced.

Case study – development in cold environments

Only: AQA, OCR A, OCR B

Svalbard, Norway	
Development opportunities	• **Mineral extraction:** mining provides over 300 jobs, boosting the local economy. • **Energy:** Svalbard aims to use geothermal energy due to being near constructive plate boundaries. • **Fishing:** the surrounding ocean is home to over 150 species of fish, supporting the fishing industry and providing food for locals. • **Tourism:** activities like glacier tours and wildlife spotting attract tourists, creating jobs and supporting the economy.
Challenges for development	• **Extreme temperatures:** winter temperatures drop below –30°C, making daily life difficult. • **Inaccessibility:** Svalbard is remote, with only one airport in Longyearbyen. Flights come from Norway and Russia, limiting access. • **Infrastructure:** buildings are specially designed with insulation to retain heat, and pipes are insulated to prevent freezing and damage.

Value of cold environments

Only: AQA, OCR A, OCR B

• **Scientific research:** these areas provide unique opportunities for scientists to study ecosystems in their natural, unimpaired state. Research in cold environments helps scientists understand global climate change.
• **Indigenous communities:** cold environments are home to Indigenous people, such as the Inuit in the Arctic, who have adapted to live sustainably in these harsh conditions. Protecting these areas helps preserve their cultures and traditional ways of life.
• **Biodiversity and habitats:** cold environments are important habitats for many species, including polar bears, penguins, seals, and unique plant species. Protecting these habitats is essential for maintaining global biodiversity.
• **Global moral responsibility:** there is a global ethical responsibility to preserve wilderness areas as a reflection of the natural world. These areas are some of the last untouched places on Earth and should be protected for future generations.

Management of cold environments

Only: AQA, OCR A, OCR B

There are several strategies to balance economic development and conservation in cold environments.
• **Use of technology:** can help reduce environmental damage while allowing for economic development. For example:
  ◦ The **Trans-Alaskan Pipeline** is a 1,300 km pipeline that transports oil from Prudhoe Bay to the port of Valdez on the Pacific Ocean. The pipeline is insulated and raised above the ground in some areas to prevent the heat of the oil from melting the permafrost. It is also designed to withstand earthquakes and allow caribou to migrate underneath it, minimising environmental impact.
• **Protected areas:** governments can designate vulnerable areas as being protected from commercial or exploitative activities that could compromise the environment. For example:
  ◦ The **National Oceanic and Atmospheric Administration (NOAA)** protects fisheries and marine habitats in Alaska, ensuring sustainable fishing practices.
  ◦ The **U.S. Department of the Interior** protects areas in northern Alaska from oil and gas developments, balancing conservation with resource extraction.
  ◦ The **Arctic National Wildlife Refuge (ANWR)** is a protected area where oil drilling is restricted to preserve biodiversity.
• **International agreements:** global cooperation is essential to protect cold environments. For example:
  ◦ **The Antarctic Treaty (1959):** an international agreement signed by twelve countries to protect Antarctica as a natural reserve for peace and science. It bans military activity, mining, and resource extraction, ensuring the continent is used only for scientific research and conservation. The treaty also promotes international collaboration in scientific studies.
• **Conservation groups:** non-governmental organizations (NGOs) work to protect cold environments and raise awareness. Conservation groups can also educate the public and lobby governments to enforce stricter environmental regulations. For example:
  ◦ **WWF (World Wildlife Fund):** campaign to protect Arctic and Antarctic ecosystems. They work to reduce the impact of climate change, prevent oil drilling, and protect endangered species like polar bears and seals.

Coastal processes

There are two types of rocks: **hard rocks** like **granite** and **limestone** are resistant to erosion. They form tall cliffs, headlands, and other prominent coastal features. By contrast, **soft rocks:** like **clay** and **sand** are weaker and erode more easily. They form low cliffs, bays, and beaches.

- **Weathering processes:**
  - **Mechanical weathering:** breaks rocks into smaller pieces. For example, **freeze-thaw weathering** occurs when water enters cracks, freezes, and expands, causing the rock to break apart over time.
  - **Chemical weathering:** rocks are broken down by chemical reactions. For example, **acid rain** reacts with minerals in rocks, causing rocks to weaken and break.
- **Mass movement:**
  - **Sliding:** large blocks of rocks slide down a cliff along a flat surface.
  - **Slumping:** saturated soil and rocks move down a curved surface, often where permeable rock lies above impermeable rock.
  - **Rock falls:** rocks break away and fall freely from a cliff due to gravity, often triggered by freeze-thaw weathering.

Sliding — slide plane

Slumping — saturated soil, stream

Rock falls — rock fragments break away, scree

- **Erosion:**
  - **Hydraulic power:** waves force air into cracks in the rock, causing pressure to build. Over time, this expands and breaks the rock apart.
  - **Abrasion:** rocks and sediment carried by waves smash against cliffs, wearing the cliff away.
  - **Attrition:** rocks and pebbles in the sea collide, breaking into smaller, smoother pieces.
- **Deposition:**
  - Occurs when the sea loses energy and drops the sediment it carried. Common in areas with constructive waves, shallow water, sheltered areas (e.g. bays), and little or no wind.

- **Transportation—longshore drift:**
  - The sediment is moved along the coast by waves.
  - **Swash** carries material up the beach at an angle (in the direction of the prevailing wind).
  - **Backwash** pulls material back into the sea at a right angle.
  - This process moves sediment along the coastline and contributes to the formation of features like spits and beaches.

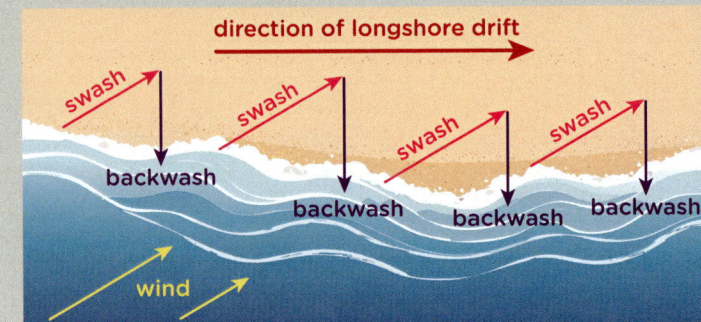

direction of longshore drift
swash — backwash
wind

Wave types and characteristics

- **Constructive waves:** low energy, strong swash, weak backwash. These waves build up beaches by depositing sediment.
- **Destructive waves:** high energy, weak swash, strong backwash. These waves erode the coastline by removing sediment.
- **Wave height and length** depend on wind strength, duration, and fetch (i.e. the distance the wind blows over water).

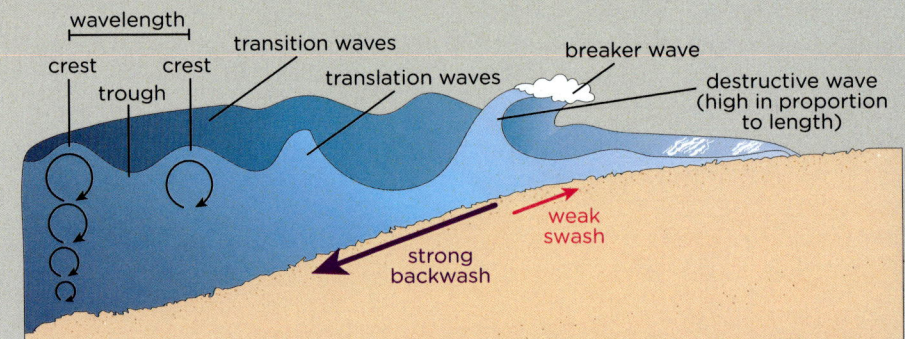

wavelength, crest, trough, crest, transition waves, translation waves, breaker wave, destructive wave (high in proportion to length), weak swash, strong backwash

Geological landforms resulting from erosion

- **Headlands and bays:**
  - Found on **discordant coastlines**, where alternating bands of hard and soft rock run perpendicular to the coast.
  - **Hard rock** (e.g. limestone, granite) resists erosion, forming **headlands** that protrudes into the sea.
  - **Soft rock** (e.g. clay, sand) erodes more easily, forming bays.
  - Headlands are exposed to high-energy waves, forming **cliffs**, **wave-cut platforms**, and **stacks**.
  - Bays are sheltered by headlands, experience low-energy waves, leading to **deposition** and the formation of **beaches**.

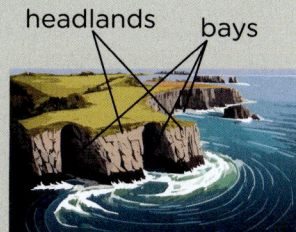
headlands   bays

- **Cliffs and wave-cut platforms**
  - **Erosion at the base:** hydraulic action and abrasion erode the base of a cliff, creating a **wave-cut notch**.
  - **Collapse:** the overhanging cliff becomes unstable and collapses due to gravity (e.g. rockfall or landslide).
  - **Retreat:** the cliff face retreats inland, leaving behind a **wave-cut platform** (a flat, rocky area exposed at low tide).
  - **Smoothing:** the wave-cut platform is smoothed over time by abrasion as pebbles grind against it.

cliff erosion and retreating
wave-cut platform   smoothing

- **Caves, arches, stacks, and stumps:**
  - **Cracks and joints:** the sea erodes weaknesses in the rock (e.g. joints, cracks, or faults) through hydraulic action, wave pounding, abrasion, and solution.
  - **Cave:** over time, the cracks expand and develops into a **cave**.
  - **Arch:** if the cave continues to erode through a headland, it forms an **arch**.
  - **Stack:** the roof of the arch collapses due to weathering and wave energy, leaving a **stack** (a tall column of rock).
  - **Stump:** the stack is further eroded by waves, eventually collapsing to form a **stump**, which is visible at low tide.

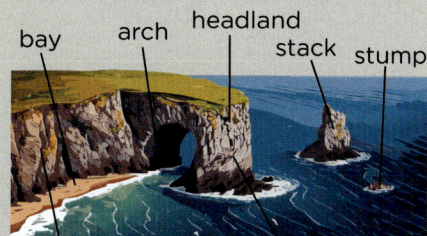
bay   arch   headland   stack   stump
soft rock (more eroded, retreats over time)   hard rock (less eroded, juts out over time)

Geological landforms resulting from deposition

- **Beaches:**
  - Constructive waves deposit **sand** or **shingle** along the coastline.
  - **Sand beaches:** found in sheltered areas with low-energy waves.
  - **Shingle beaches:** found in areas with high-energy waves, where sand is washed away, leaving behind pebbles.
  - Example: the **south coast of England** has pebble beaches due to destructive waves removing sand.
- **Sand dunes:**
  - **Embryo dunes:** forms near the sea when sand is deposited and trapped by obstacles like vegetation.
  - **Growth:** marram grass and other vegetation grow on dunes, stabilising dunes with their long roots.
  - **Organic matter:** decaying vegetation adds nutrients to the sand, allowing more plants to colonise.
  - **Mature dunes:** older dunes, further from the sea, may support shrubs and trees.
- **Spits:**
  - **Longshore drift:** sediment is transported along the coast by longshore drift.
  - **Change in coastline:** when the coastline changes direction (e.g. at a river mouth), sediment is deposited, forming a spit.
  - **Extension:** the spit extends out into the sea, with longshore drift continuing to deposit material.
  - **Hooked end:** strong winds and wave action curve the end of the spit, forming a **hooked end**.
  - **Salt marsh:** sheltered water behind the spit allows salt marshes to form, creating ideal habitats for wildlife (e.g. Dawlish Warren Spit, Devon).

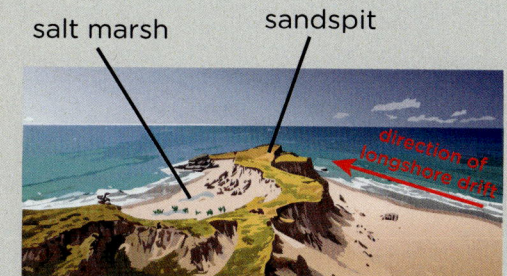
salt marsh   sandspit
direction of longshore drift

- **Bars:**
  - A **bar** forms when longshore drift continues depositing sediment across a bay, connecting two headlands.
  - This creates a **ridge of sand or shingle** that blocks off the bay, forming a **lagoon** behind it. (e.g. Slapton Sands Bar, Devon).

Management strategies for coastal landscapes

SNAPREVISE

Management strategies to protect coastlines

Hard engineering management strategies		
	Benefits	**Costs**
Sea walls	• Very effective barrier • Top of wall can be a walkway	• Very expensive • Eyesore
Rock armour	• Cheap to construct • Can be used as for fishing	• Different rock type may be an eyesore • Can be dangerous if not maintained
Gabions	• Cheaper option • Stabilises cliffs and blends in over time	• Short lifespan and needs maintenance • Eyesore
Groynes	• Cheaper option • Builds beaches	• Increases erosion downstream • Needs maintenance

Soft engineering management strategies		
	Benefits	**Costs**
Beach nourishment & reprofiling	• Environmentally friendly • Amenity for tourism • Cheap, easy to maintain	• Expensive initial costs • People can't use the beach during maintenance
Dune regeneration	• Looks natural • Increases biodiversity	• Time-consuming • Easily damaged by storms

Managed retreat management strategies		
	Benefits	**Costs**
Coastal realignment	• Controlled process where the sea is allowed to flood or erode low-lying areas to reduce pressure on other parts of the coastline. • Embankments are built further inland to protect valuable land (e.g. farms). • Flooded areas can create new habitats like salt marshes, which function as natural barriers to absorb wave energy. • Cheaper and more sustainable than hard engineering.	• Land is lost to the sea, which can affect farmers and property owners. • Relocation of people and infrastructure required.

Case study – features of coastlines

Dorset coastline, England	
Swanage Bay (headland and bay)	• The area around Swanage is a discordant coastline, made of alternating bands of hard rock (chalk and limestone) and soft rock (clay and sand). • Soft rock erodes faster, forming bays like Swanage Bay. • Hard rock erodes slower, forming headlands like Ballard Point and Durlston Head.
Old Harry Rocks	• Old Harry Rocks are made of chalk (hard rock) that sticks out into the sea. • Erosion (hydraulic action and abrasion) has created features like stacks (Old Harry) and stumps (collapsed stacks). • The chalk is exposed to high-energy waves, making it vulnerable to further erosion.
Chesil Beach-Bar	• Chesil Beach is a bar formed by longshore drift, where sediment has been deposited over time. It connects the mainland to the Isle of Portland, behind which is a lagoon.

Case study – managing coastlines

Holderness coastline	
Key details	• Location: north-east England • Erosion rate: retreats at 1–2 metres per year, one of the fastest eroding coastlines in Europe
Reasons for management	• **Geology:** the cliffs are made of soft clay, which erodes quickly, especially when saturated by rain. • **Longshore drift:** strong prevailing winds move material southwards, reducing beach size and exposing cliffs.
Management strategies	• **Groynes:** two groynes were built to trap sediment and create a wider beach, protecting the cliffs from waves. • **Rock armour:** large boulders were placed at the base of the cliffs to absorb wave energy and reduce erosion.
Effects and conflicts	• **Tourism:** increased litter, hazards, and demand for facilities, increasing pressure on local infrastructure. • **Sustainability:** rising sea levels mean future defences must consider long-term sustainability (groynes causing increased erosion down the coast at Mappleton).

Profile of rivers

The **long profile** of a river illustrates how the gradient (slope) of the river changes from its source to mouth. The **cross profile** of a river refers to the shape of a river valley and channel at different points along its course. It changes due to variations in erosion, transportation, and deposition.

- **Upper course:** (near the source, often in upland areas) steep gradient, uneven surface, and high energy focused on vertical erosion.
  - **Valley shape:** narrow, steep-sided V-shaped valleys.
  - **Processes:** vertical erosion (with minimal lateral erosion) caused by:
    - **Abrasion:** rocks and sediment scrape the riverbed and banks.
    - **Attrition:** rocks collide and breakdown into smaller pieces.
    - **Hydraulic action:** the force of water breaks down the rock.
  - **Channel:** narrow, shallow, large, angular bedload (rocks and sediment).
- **Middle course:** gradient becomes less steep, and the river begins to meander. Both lateral and vertical erosion occurs.
  - **Valley shape:** wider and shallower valley with gentler slopes.
  - **Processes:** increased **lateral erosion** widens the valley; some **deposition** occurs on the inside bends of meanders; **transportation** of sediment is more efficient due to increased discharge and velocity.
  - **Channel:** wider and deeper, with smaller, more rounded sediment.
- **Lower course:** (near the mouth) gentle gradient, with deposition dominating over erosion as the river flows over flat land.
  - **Valley shape:** very wide and flat valley with floodplains.
  - **Processes:** deposition more common due to lower energy levels; minimal erosion; formation of levees, deltas, and oxbow lakes.
  - **Channel:** very wide and deep, with fine sediment (silt and clay) being transported and deposited.

Fluvial processes

- **Erosion:** involves the wearing away of riverbeds and banks by the river's energy and materials it carries.
  - **Abrasion:** rock fragments carried by the river collide with the sides and bed of the river, eroding the rock.
  - **Attrition:** rocks and pebbles carried by the river collide with each other, breaking into smaller, smoother, and rounder pieces.
  - **Hydraulic action:** the force of water striking the riverbanks compresses air into cracks, causing the rock to break.
  - **Solution erosion:** minerals in the rocks (e.g. limestone) are dissolved by the slightly acidic river water.
- **Transportation:** refers to how the river moves material downstream.
  - **Traction:** large rocks and boulders are rolled along the riverbed by the force of the water.
  - **Saltation:** pebbles and stones bounce along the riverbed, as they are too heavy to remain suspended.
  - **Suspension:** fine particles (e.g. silt and clay) are carried within the water, making it look muddy.
  - **Solution transportation:** dissolved minerals are carried in the water, invisible to the eye.
- **Deposition:** occurs when the river loses energy and drops its load.
  - This happens when the river slows down (e.g. in the lower course or during low flow) or when the material is too heavy for the river to carry (e.g. large rocks or boulders).
  - Deposition is common in the **lower course** where rivers form features like floodplains, levees, and deltas.

Hydrographs

A **hydrograph** shows the relationship between **precipitation** (rainfall) and **discharge** (water flow in a river) over time. Hydrographs are useful for **flood prediction** by predicting the likelihood of flooding by analysing how quickly a river responds to rainfall, and for **flood warnings** to issue alerts and plan evacuations.

The key components of a hydrograph are:
- **Peak discharge:** the maximum volume of water held in the river channel during a storm.
- **Peak rainfall:** the maximum volume of rainfall recorded during the storm.
- **Lag time:** the time between peak rainfall and peak discharge. A shorter lag time increases flood risk.
- **Rising limb:** the part of the hydrograph that shows the increase in river discharge after rainfall.
- **Recessional limb:** the decrease in river discharge after the point of peak flow.

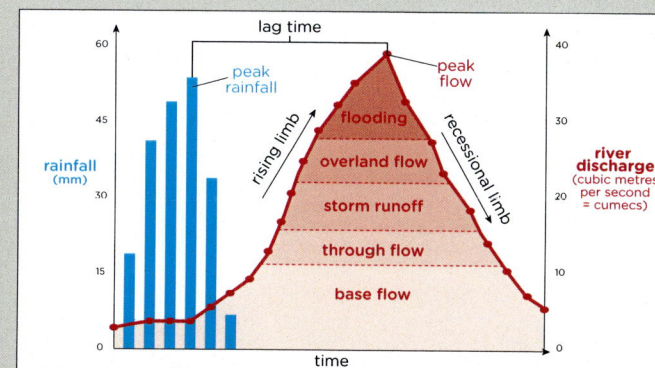

Fluvial landform processes

Fluvial landforms resulting from erosion

- **Interlocking spurs:** are found in the **upper course** of a river where the river flows around ridges of hard rock, creating a zig-zag pattern. Valleys are steep-sided and narrow, with a **V-shaped profile**, formed when:
  1. In the upper course, the river has **low energy** and erodes vertically through **abrasion** and **hydraulic action**.
  2. When the river meets hard, resistant rock, it cannot erode it easily.
  3. Instead, the river bends around the hard rock, leaving **interlocking spurs** of land that project into the valley.

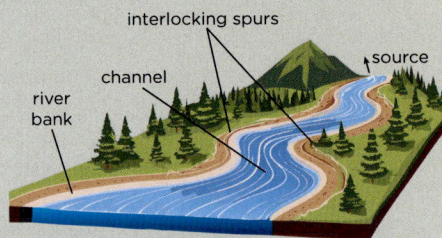

- **Waterfalls and gorges:** waterfalls are steep vertical drops in the river's course, often with a plunge pool at the base. Gorges are narrow, steep-sided valleys formed as waterfalls retreat upstream. They are formed when:
  1. A river flows over a band of **hard, resistant rock** that lies over **soft rock**.
  2. The **soft rock** is eroded faster due to **abrasion** and **hydraulic action**, creating an **undercut** beneath the hard rock.
  3. Over time, the **hard rock** becomes unsupported and collapses into the plunge pool.
  4. This process repeats, causing the waterfall to **retreat upstream**.
  5. The retreating waterfall leaves behind a **steep-sided gorge**.

Fluvial landforms resulting from erosion and deposition

- **Meanders:** large bends in the river, typically found in the **middle/lower courses**. The outer bend has a **river cliff** due to erosion, while the inner bend has a **slip-off slope** due to deposition. The are formed when:
  - The river flows faster on the **outer bend** of a meander, increasing **erosion** through **hydraulic action** and **abrasion**.
  - **Lateral erosion** undercuts the riverbank, forming a **river cliff**.
  - On the **inner bend**, the water flows slower due to **friction**, leading to **deposition** of material like sand and shingle, forming a **slip-off slope**.
- **Ox-bow lakes:** a crescent-shaped lake formed when a meander is cut off from the main channel, found in the **lower course** of a river. They are formed when:
  - **Lateral erosion** on the outer bends of a meander causes the bends to move closer, narrowing the **meander neck**.
  - In a **flood** the river cuts through the neck creating a **straight channel**.
  - **Deposition** seals off the old meander, leaving an **ox-bow lake**.

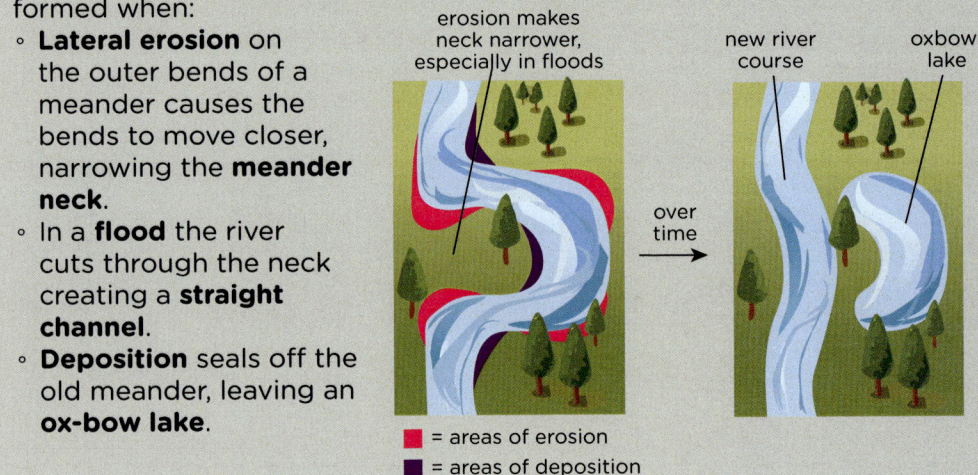

Fluvial landforms resulting from deposition

- **Levees:** are natural embankments along the sides of a river's flood-prone lower course. During flood events, the river overflows onto the floodplain, depositing heavy sediment first (e.g. coarse sand and gravel) at the river's edge. Over time, repeated flooding builds up these deposits, creating raised ridges known as levees that contain the river within its channel during high-flow events, reducing the risk of flooding.
- **Floodplains:** a broad, flat expanse of land adjacent to a river formed by the deposition of alluvium (fine particles of silt, clay, and sand) during floods. When a river overflows, its velocity drops significantly, allowing finer sediments to settle across the valley floor. Over many flood cycles, these deposits build up to create fertile, level land, providing nutrient-rich soils for agriculture and supporting diverse ecosystems.
- **Estuaries:** a partially enclosed coastal body of water where freshwater from a river meets and mixes with ocean saltwater. As the river approaches the sea, its flow slows dramatically, causing sediment carried from upstream to settle and form mudflats which can be colonised by salt-tolerant vegetation, leading to the development of salt marshes. Estuaries are highly productive environments that support a wide range of wildlife between river and marine ecosystems.

Management strategies to protect coastlines

Hard engineering management strategies		
	Benefits	**Costs**
Dams and reservoirs	• Provide hydroelectric power of water through turbines • Attracts tourists	• Extremely expensive (e.g. Kilder Dam cost £167 million) • Settlements and habitats flooded
Straightening	• Can hold more water	• Speeding rivers creates flooding downstream • High maintenance due to dredging
Embankments	• Increases capacity, reducing flood risk • Creates walkways	• Eyesore/looks artificial • Leads to more serious flooding if embankment fails • Expensive to construct
Flood relief channels	• Removes excess water from rivers to reduce flooding in towns. • Opportunities for recreation (e.g. fishing, walking)	• Expensive to construct • Habitats disturbed • If water levels rise, relief channels can flood

Soft engineering management strategies		
	Benefits	**Costs**
Flood warning and preparations	• People have time to protect property	• Need for monitoring equipment and science expertise • Does not prevent flooding • Some may not receive warnings
Flood plain zoning	• Reduces additional impermeable surface coverage • Less damage, so fewer insurance claims	• Restricts economic development in the area • House shortages if land is not used
River restoration	• Reduced flood risk	• Expensive • Time-consuming

Factors affecting flood risk

- **Physical factors:**
  - **Heavy precipitation:** exceeds infiltration capacity, causing surface runoff.
  - **Prolonged precipitation:** saturates the soil, reducing infiltration and increasing runoff.
  - **Sudden snowmelt or storms:** can cause flash flooding
  - **Geology:** impermeable rocks (e.g. granite or clay) prevent infiltration and increase runoff, while permeable rocks (e.g. sandstone or chalk) allow water to soak in, reducing flood risk.
  - **Steep slopes:** cause water to flow rapidly downhill reducing infiltration time and increasing flood risk.
  - **Vegetation:** dense flora increases interception and transpiration, reducing runoff, whereas sparse or absent vegetation leads to erosion and faster surface flow.
- **Human factors:**
  - **Land use:** bare soil from agriculture or deforestation transfers water quickly, and ploughing slopes create tunnels (streams downhill).
  - **Urbanisation:** lack of vegetation and impermeable surfaces (e.g. concrete, tarmac) results in overland flow and little absorption.
  - **River management:** channel straightening, levees, embankments, dams, and reservoirs can all help manage or divert flood risks.
  - **Climate change:** leads to more frequent and intense storms, increasing rainfall and wetter seasons, increasing the likelihood of floods.

Case study – flood relief projects

Jubilee River flood relief channel	
Key details	• Created to prevent future flooding to towns at risk of damage by taking excess water from the Thames. • Completed in 2002 and cost £110 million.
Social details	• Protection of more affluent regions at the expense of poorer areas.
Economic issues	• Most expensive flood relief scheme in the UK.
Environmental issues	• Algae growth affects aquatic life, and concrete weirs are unattractive to locals and tourists.

Glacial landscapes

Glacial processes

Only:
AQA, Edexcel A

- **Plucking:** loose bedrock freezes and is pulled away as the glacier moves, creating a jagged surface.
- **Abrasion:** rocks at the bottom of the glacier scrape and smooth bedrock.
- **Freeze-thaw weathering:** water enters cracks in a rock, freezes, and expands, breaking the rock apart.
- **Bulldozing:** occurs when the glacier's snout (front) pushes loose material (e.g. rocks, soil) downhill.
- **Rotational slip:** occurs when meltwater at the base of a glacier reduces friction, allowing the glacier to slide downhill.
- **Glacial till:** unsorted material deposited by a glacier.
- **Outwash:** sediment (sand, gravel, silt) deposited by meltwater from a glacier, usually sorted and found in outwash plains.

Land use conflicts

Only:
AQA, Edexcel A

- **Tourism vs. Farming:** tourists may damage walls, trample crops, or disturb livestock, while farmers may restrict access to land, frustrating tourists.
- **Tourism vs. Quarrying:** quarrying damages the landscape, reducing its appeal to tourists. Noise and dust from quarries may disturb visitors.
- **Tourism vs. Conservation:** overcrowding and footpath erosion damage fragile environments. Litter and pollution harm wildlife and habitats.
- **Farming vs. Conservation:** overgrazing by sheep can reduce biodiversity and harm ecosystems. Conservationists may want to restore ecosystems and biodiversity, which can conflict with farming practices.
- **Development vs. Conservation:** building infrastructure (e.g. roads, car parks) for tourism can harm natural habitats. Renewable energy projects (e.g. wind farms) may conflict with preserving the area's natural beauty.

Economic activities in glaciated upland areas

Only:
AQA, Edexcel A

	Advantages	Disadvantages
Tourism	• Provides jobs in hotels, restaurants, and outdoor activities • Boosts local economies with tourism spending	• Overcrowding, traffic congestion, and environmental damage (e.g. footpath erosion)
Farming	• Maintains traditional farming practices and rural communities	• Farming can conflict with tourism (e.g. walkers disturbing livestock) • Overgrazing to provide food can lead to soil erosion and loss of biodiversity
Forestry	• Provides timber for construction and paper industries • Jobs in rural areas	• Conflicts with tourism as forests block views
Quarrying	• Provides raw materials for construction and industry • Jobs in rural areas	• Scars the landscape with noise and dust, and can harm wildlife • Conflicts with tourism as it reduces natural beauty.

Case study – glacial areas

Only:
AQA, Edexcel A

The Lake District	
Attractions for tourists	• **Natural attractions:** scenic landscapes include ribbon lakes (e.g. Windermere), U-shaped valleys (e.g. Langdale Valley), and mountains (e.g. Scafell Pike). • **Outdoor activities:** hiking, cycling, and water sports. • **Cultural attractions:** historic sites include Beatrix Potter's house and Wordsworth's Dove Cottage.
Impacts of tourism	• **Social impacts:** tourism supports local services and jobs, but overcrowding (e.g. Ambleside) reduces residents' quality of life and decreases affordability. • **Economic impacts:** £1 million spent annually by tourists, but many jobs are seasonal or low-paid. Heavy reliance on tourism makes the economy vulnerable to fluctuations in visitor numbers. • **Environmental impacts:** footpath erosion (e.g. Scafell Pike), litter, and traffic congestion all damage the area.
Strategies to manage impacts of tourism	• **Traffic:** park-and-ride schemes to reduce congestion. • **Footpaths:** stone pitching (laying stones to create a durable path) repairs erosion on busy routes. • **Litter:** bins, signage, and volunteer clean-ups promote responsible behaviour.

Glacial landform processes

Glacial landforms resulting from erosion

Only: AQA, Edexcel A

- **Corries:** bowl-shaped hollow with a steep back wall and a raised lip at the front. These are formed when snow collects in a hollow on a mountainside and compresses into ice over time. The glacier moves due to gravity, eroding the hollow through **plucking** (ice pulls rocks away from the back wall); abrasion and rotational slip causes the hollow to deepen.
  - **Freeze-thaw weathering** breaks up rocks on the back wall, steepening it further. When the glacier melts, the hollow is left behind, often with a **tarn** (small lake).
- **Arêtes:** a sharp, narrow ridge between two corries. These are formed when two corries form back-to-back or side-by-side on a mountain. As the glaciers erode the corries through plucking and abrasion, the ridge between it becomes narrower.
  - **Freeze-thaw weathering** sharpens the ridge further.
- **Pyramidal peaks:** sharp, pointed mountain peaks with steep sides. These are formed when three or more corries form around a single mountain and glaciers erode the mountain on all sides through plucking and abrasion.
  - **Freeze-thaw weathering** sharpens the peak into a pyramid shape.
- **Truncated spurs:** steep, cliff-like edges where interlocking spurs (from a river valley) have been cut off. These are formed in a river valley when interlocking spurs form as the river bends around hard rock. When a glacier moves through the valley, it erodes through the spurs using plucking and abrasion. This results in steep, truncated (cut-off) edges.
- **Glacial troughs (U-shaped valleys):** wide, flat valley floor with steep sides; often much straighter than a river valley. These are formed when a glacier moves through a V-shaped river valley and erodes it through plucking and abrasion, making it deeper, wider, and straighter. After the glacier melts, a U-shaped valley is left behind.
- **Ribbon lakes:** long, narrow lake found in a glacial trough. These are formed when a glacier erodes softer rock deeper than hard rock, creating a hollow. When the glacier melts, the hollow fills with meltwater, forming a ribbon lake.
- **Hanging valleys:** smaller valleys that hang above the main glacial trough; often containing waterfalls where the smaller valley meets the main valley. These are formed when smaller tributary glaciers erode less deep than the main glacier due to carrying less ice. After the glaciers melt, smaller valleys are left 'hanging' above the main valley.

Glacial landforms resulting from transportation and deposition

Only: AQA, Edexcel A

- **Erratics:** large boulders deposited in an area of different rock type. They appear incongruous compared to the surrounding geology. They are formed when glaciers pick up rocks from one area as they move. These rocks are transported long distances and deposited when the glacier melts.
- **Drumlins:** smooth, elongated hills made of glacial till (unsorted material). They are steep at one end (stoss) and gently sloping at the other (lee). They are formed when glaciers deposit unsorted material (known as till) as they lose energy. As the glacier continues to move, it reshapes the deposited material into a streamlined, elongated hill called a **drumlin**. The **steep stoss end** (upstream end) faces the direction from which the glacier originated, while the **tapered lee end** (downstream end) points in the direction the glacier was moving.
- **Moraines:**
  - **Lateral moraine:** ridge of material deposited along the sides of a glacier. These are formed when rocks and debris fall from the valley walls onto the glacier and are deposited by freeze-thawing.
  - **Medial moraine:** ridge of material running down the centre of a glacier. These are formed when two glaciers meet, their lateral moraines combine to form a medial moraine.
  - **Terminal moraine:** ridge of material deposited at the glacier's furthest point. These are formed when the glacier pushes material ahead of it through bulldozing, depositing this material at its snout when it melts.
  - **Ground moraine:** material unevenly spread across the valley floor. These are formed when material is deposited as the glacier melts and retreats.

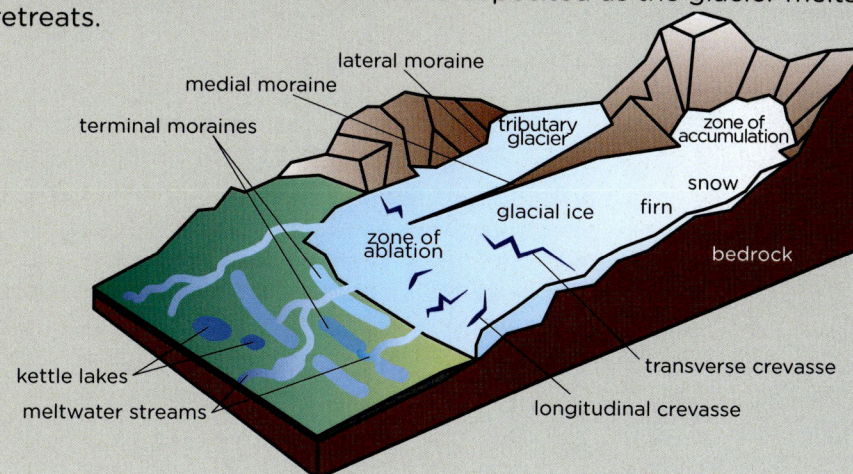

Labels: lateral moraine, medial moraine, terminal moraines, tributary glacier, zone of accumulation, snow, firn, glacial ice, zone of ablation, bedrock, kettle lakes, meltwater streams, transverse crevasse, longitudinal crevasse

Key terms

- **Urbanisation**: is when more people move to towns and cities, causing it to grow. Urbanisation is increasing faster in LICs (Low-Income Countries) than HICs (High-Income Countries) because most HICs are already urbanised. By 2050, India, China, and Nigeria will account for 37% of global urbanisation growth.
- **Push factors** are reasons people leave an area (e.g. lack of jobs, poor living conditions), whereas **pull factors** are reasons people move to an area (e.g. better jobs, healthcare, education).
- **Megacities**: cities with over 10 million people (e.g. London, Dhaka, Tokyo).

Case study – urbanisation opportunities and challenges

Rio de Janeiro, Brazil	
Location and importance of city	• Location: south-east coast of Brazil • Population: 6.211 million people (2022) • Nationally important trading port and oil industry and is internationally significant as a major tourist destination.
Opportunities from urban growth	• **Healthcare:** medical teams visit favelas, improving life expectancy and reducing infant mortality. • **Education:** volunteer teachers and grants for schools help children stay in education. • **Water supply:** 95% of favelas had mains water by 2014 after building treatment plants. • **Energy:** new power lines and a nuclear generator reduce blackouts caused by illegal tapping of electricity. • **Economic:** Rio provides 6% of Brazil's jobs to industries like oil, retail, and tourism.
Challenges from urban growth	• **Waste disposal:** narrow streets in favelas prevent rubbish collection, leading to pollution and diseases like cholera. • **Traffic congestion:** Rio de Janeiro experiences traffic jams in the city centre as many people travel by car because it is considered safer. However, this contributes to air pollution. The Teleférico do Alemão cable cars provide residents with a free return ticket daily, offering a 6-minute commute time. • **Water pollution:** sewage from favelas pollutes rivers, harming aquatic life.

Case study – urban change in the UK

All specs except: CIE, Pearson IGCSE

Bristol, UK	
Location and importance of city	• Location: south-west England. • Population: 483,000 people (2024) • High-tech industries; 2015 Green Capital award winner.
Opportunities from urban change	• **Cultural mix:** community events and social harmony. • **Recreation:** the aim is to plant trees so that tree canopy will cover 20% of the city with trees by 2035. • **Employment:** jobs in low-carbon industries. • **Transport:** bio-buses powered by food and sewage waste. • **Urban greening:** 27% of the city is a wildlife network, with plans to make Bristol an urban nature reserve.
Social challenges from urban change	Inequalities between two areas (Filwood and Stoke Bishop): • **Housing:** Filwood has poorly insulated homes, while 81% of Stoke Bishop homes are owner-occupied. • **Education:** only 36% of Filwood students get grades 5-9 at GCSE, compared to 94% in Stoke Bishop. • **Health:** life expectancy 78 in Filwood vs 83 in Stoke Bishop. • **Employment:** 1/3 of 16-24-year-olds in Filwood are unemployed, compared to 3% in Stoke Bishop.
Environmental challenges from urban change	• **Dereliction:** abandoned properties in Stokes Croft. • **Waste disposal:** 1/2 million tons of waste annually. • **Brownfield vs. greenfield site building:** brownfield sites have easier planning as there is existing infrastructure, whereas greenfield sites have more garden space but building on them may harm the countryside. • **Urban sprawl:** expands into rural areas, destroying ecosystems and increasing pollution.
Urban regeneration	**Temple Quarter Project:** • Deemed necessary to address the lack of green spaces, low income, poor transport options, and absence of business opportunities. • Electrified train tracks for faster, quieter, and eco-friendly transport. • A £200 million university campus to teach tech skills. • Sustainable buildings like Glass Wharf with tinted windows to reduce energy use.

Urban sustainability

- **Water conservation:** involves reducing water usage through efficient fixtures, rainwater harvesting, greywater recycling, and fixing leaks.
- **Energy conservation:** involves using energy-efficient appliances, LED lighting, renewable energy sources (e.g. solar panels), and better insulation in buildings to reduce energy demand.
- **Waste recycling:** involves collecting, processing, and reusing materials like paper, plastic, glass, and metal to reduce landfill use. This promotes composting of organic waste, encourages waste separation at the source, and conserves natural resources.
- **Creating green space:** refers to developing parks, community gardens, green roofs, and street trees. Benefits include improved air quality, reduced urban heat island effect, support for biodiversity, and enhanced mental and physical wellbeing for residents.

Case study – urban sustainability

Freiburg, Germany	
Water conservation	• Rainwater is collected and recycled for drinking and flushing toilets.
Energy conservation	• Aims to be 100% renewable by 2050.
Waste recycling	• Separate bins for recycling.
Green spaces	• Parks for relaxation and wellbeing.
Transport	• 70% of people live within 500m of a tram stop. • 400km of cycle paths encourage healthy and eco-friendly travel.

Measures of development

Development: refers to the progress of a country as it becomes more economically and technologically advanced.
- **Social measures of development:**
  ◦ **Birth and death rate:** the number of live births and deaths per 1,000 people. Reflects healthcare, food, and water availability but can be misleading in countries with many elderly people.
  ◦ **Life expectancy:** the average age a person is expected to live.
  ◦ **Infant mortality:** the number of children who die before their first birthday per 1,000 live births.
  ◦ **People per doctor:** shows availability of medical training/healthcare.
  ◦ **Adult literacy rate:** the percentage of adults who can read and write.
  ◦ **Access to clean water:** indicates if a country has invested in safe water systems to prevent diseases from contaminated water.
- **Economic measures of development:**
  ◦ **Gross National Income (GNI) per person:** shows the average income of a country's population.
  ◦ **HDI (Human Development Index):** combines data on income, life expectancy, and education to give a score between 0 and 1, with 0 meaning a poor level of development.
- **Limitations of development measures:**
  ◦ Birth/death rates can be misleading; other measures are needed to contextualise what these rates really mean.
  ◦ Life expectancy data may be unreliable in LICs (low-income countries) due to high infant mortality caused by poor healthcare.
  ◦ GNI per person data can be sensitive; people may not report accurately.

Demographic Transition Model (DMI)

- The DMI shows how population growth and composition change over time as a country develops economically, helping governments and NGOs understand and predict population trends and development challenges.
- However, it is mostly based on historical trends in Western Europe and does not apply universally to all regions or cultures.

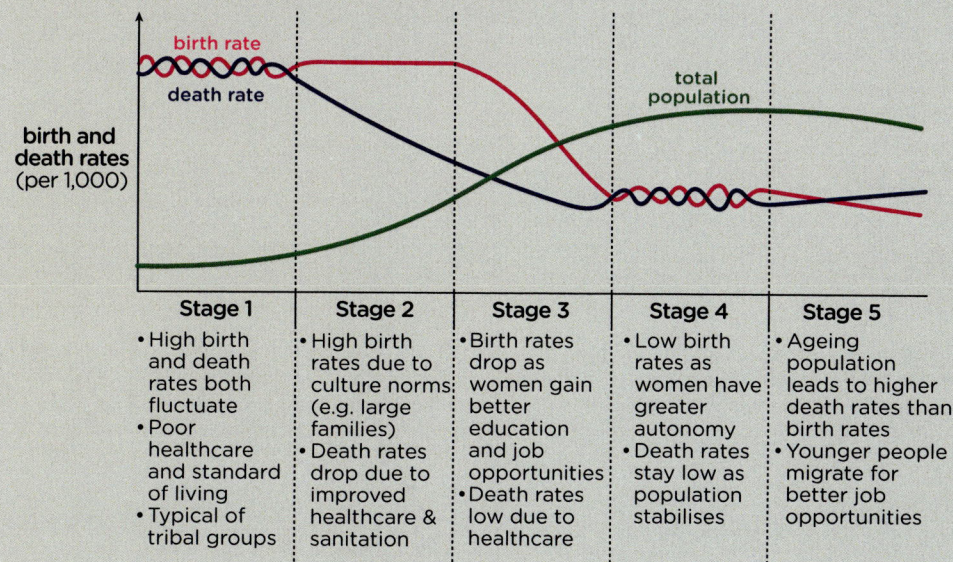

Stage 1	Stage 2	Stage 3	Stage 4	Stage 5
•High birth and death rates both fluctuate •Poor healthcare and standard of living •Typical of tribal groups	•High birth rates due to culture norms (e.g. large families) •Death rates drop due to improved healthcare & sanitation	•Birth rates drop as women gain better education and job opportunities •Death rates low due to healthcare	•Low birth rates as women have greater autonomy •Death rates stay low as population stabilises	•Ageing population leads to higher death rates than birth rates •Younger people migrate for better job opportunities

27

SNAPREVISE

Strategies to reduce the development gap

- **Investment:** TNCs or HICs invest in infrastructure and create jobs.
- **Industrial development:** expands employment opportunities and boosts the economy.
- **Tourism:** creates legal jobs, and workers pay taxes that support the economy.
- **Fairtrade:** ensures farmers in LICs are paid fairly for their produce.
- **Debt relief:** cancelling debts allows countries to invest in development.
- **Microfinance loans:** small loans help individuals start businesses and improve livelihoods.

Case study – tourism development

Tourism in Jamaica	
Key details	• Jamaica, located in the Caribbean, is known for its rich culture and heritage, which attracts tourists.
Benefits	• The tourism industry provides jobs for 200,000 local people, reducing unemployment. • Improved infrastructure for tourists (e.g. roads, airports) also benefits locals, improving their quality of life. • Increased tax revenue from tourism contributes to Jamaica's economy and development.
Costs	• Over-tourism contributes to beach erosion, coral reef damage, and strain on natural resources. • Heavy reliance on tourism makes Jamaica vulnerable to global economic shifts and natural disasters.

Types of aid

Aid is voluntary help provided by individuals, organisations, or governments to improve quality of life. The types of aid include:
- **Short-term aid:** immediate help after disasters to address urgent needs.
- **Long-term aid:** ongoing support to improve living standards over time.
- **Official Development Assistance (ODA):** aid funded by taxes and government organisations.
- **Bilateral aid:** aid given from one country to another.
- **Multilateral aid:** aid provided by multiple countries or organisations.
- **Tied aid:** aid with conditions attached (e.g. buying goods from a donor country).

Uneven development

- Uneven economic development refers to the unequal distribution of wealth and resources between countries and regions, often split into **high-income** (e.g. UK, US, Australia), **middle-income** (e.g. Mexico, China, Brazil), and **low-income** (e.g. Sudan, Uganda, Afghanistan) categories.

Causes	Consequences

• **Physical factors:**
  ○ Landlocked countries struggle with trade.
  ○ Extreme weather (e.g. storms, droughts, floods) damages infrastructure and reduces trade and tourism.
  ○ Water shortages or unhygienic water causes health issues.
• **Economic factors:**
  ○ Poverty limits income and opportunities, reducing investment in infrastructure and development.
  ○ Poor education levels limit earning potential and economic productivity.
  ○ Some countries are disproportionately exploited by globalisation (e.g. Global South producing cheap goods for HICs).
• **Historical factors:**
  ○ Civil wars damage land and reduce food production.
  ○ Colonisation exploited resources in LICs, leaving them with fewer resources to develop.
  ○ Unstable sociopolitical circumstances disrupts infrastructure and education, and can deter investment that would help the country develop.
	• **Wealth disparities:**
	  ○ LICs, like many in Africa, hold only 1% of global wealth despite having 12% of the world's population.
	  ○ Some countries are heavily dependent on aid and lack sustainable economies.
	• **Health disparities:**
	  ○ LICs lack access to healthcare, leading to deaths from diseases like malaria and tuberculosis.
	  ○ HICs experience deaths from chronic conditions like diabetes.
	  ○ LICs tend to have low life expectancy and high mortality.
	  ○ Underfunded health services lead to increased deaths by preventable disease.
	• **Migration:**
	  ○ People migrate to HICs for better opportunities or to escape conflict.
	  ○ People move from rural to urban areas even if cities are overcrowded which can create slums and 'brain drains.'

Case study – effects of rapid economic development

	Nigeria
Key details	• **Location**: Nigeria is an NEE (Newly Emerging Economy) in West Africa with a population of approximately 184 million people.
Political context	• Nigeria experienced political instability, including a civil war (1967–1970). Elections became more stable and democratic in 2011 and 2015.
Social context	• Nigeria is a **multi-cultural, multi-faith society**, but this diversity has caused regional conflicts. • Groups like **Boko Haram** have caused violence, forcing **500,000 people to flee** their homes.
Cultural context	• Nigeria has a rich culture, including a thriving music, literature, and film industry (e.g. Nollywood). • The Nigerian **football team** has won the African Cup of Nations three times.
Environmental context	• In the south, high tropical rainfall supports crops like **rubber, palm oil, and cocoa.** • In the north, less rainfall leads to grasslands, suitable for **cotton farming**.
Changing industrial structure	• Previously, Nigeria's economy was based on agriculture. Now, 50% of the economy comes from manufacturing and services (e.g. telecommunications, Nollywood, retail). A growing manufacturing industry has increased foreign investment and created more employment opportunities.

Example of a transnational company (TNC): Shell Oil	Shell Oil is a transnational company (TNC) with headquarters in the Netherlands but with major operations in Nigeria to capitalise on: low taxes, cheap labour, limited workers' rights, and fewer environmental laws
	• Advantages for Nigeria:
	  ◦ **Employment:** Shell Oil has hired 65,000 Nigerian workers, with 90% of employees being Nigerian
	  ◦ **Infrastructure development:** TNCs invest in the host country's infrastructure, such as roads and facilities, which benefits the local population.
	  ◦ **Tax revenue:** Shell has paid £20 billion in corporation tax, which the government can use to improve services and support Nigerian citizens.
	• Disadvantages for Nigeria:
	  ◦ **Poor working conditions:** workers often face unsafe and unfair conditions with limited legal recourse.
	  ◦ **Oil theft:** exposed gas and oil pipelines are vulnerable to theft, causing economic losses.
	  ◦ **Profit leakage:** most profits are sent back to the TNC headquarters in HICs, rather than being reinvested in Nigeria.
	  ◦ **Environmental damage:** the 2008 oil spill in Bodo polluted water supplies, deprived locals of food, and harmed aquatic life.

Changing global relationships	• In **2013**, Nigeria contributed the **5th largest number of troops** to the UN peacekeeping force. • Growing links with **China**, including significant investment in infrastructure projects.
Examples of aid	• **USA**: Provides aid to educate and protect Nigerians from **HIV/AIDS**. • **EU and UNICEF**: Provide funding and support for development projects.
Environmental impacts of economic development	• **Oil spills:** in the Niger Delta (e.g. Bodo, 2008) **polluted water supplies,** harmed aquatic life, and reduced fish availability as a food source. Locals were exposed to **toxic chemicals**, **unhygienic water**, and food shortages. • **Deforestation:** across Nigeria, **80% of forests** have been cut down, increasing CO_2 **levels,** and contributing to climate change. • **Industrial pollution:** harmful gases released by industries contribute to **global warming**. • **Toxic waste:** toxic chemicals released into sewers risk human health.
Effects of economic development on quality of life	• Improved access to healthcare leads to higher life expectancy and reduction in illness as people receive better medical treatment and preventative care. • Increased job opportunities provide individuals with a higher income, allowing them to afford a healthier diet and better healthcare services, which enhances their quality of life. • Developments in infrastructure, which allow access to clean water and reliable electricity, improve living conditions by reducing the spread of waterborne diseases and supporting essential services like education and healthcare.

Causes of economic change in the UK
All specs except: CIE, Pearson IGCSE

- **Deindustrialisation:** the decline of industrial activity due to economic or social changes, leading to lower income and unemployment. This has led to the decline of traditional industries:
  - During the **Industrial Revolution**, the **secondary sector** (manufacturing) dominated.
  - The **primary sector** (e.g. farming, mining) declined due to the increased use of **machinery**.
  - In the **1960s**, manufacturing declined due to **mechanisation** and **competition from abroad**.
  - Growth in the **tertiary sector** (e.g. public services, finance) and, since the **1980s**, the rise of the **quaternary sector** (e.g. research, IT).
- **Globalisation:** the world becoming more **interconnected** through **trade** and **cultural exchange**, leading to growth in the **tertiary** and **quaternary sectors**, as the UK focuses on **services** and high-tech industries.
- **Government policies:**
  - EU membership (pre-Brexit): allowed **free trade** and access to a large market, boosting industries like **finance** and manufacturing.
  - Support for high-tech industries: government funding for **science parks**, **business parks**, and **research** has encouraged the growth of **high-tech industries**.

Moving towards a post-industrial economy
All specs except: CIE, Pearson IGCSE

- **Information Technology (IT):**
  - The UK is a global leader in IT, attracting **overseas business investment**.
  - Computers can store and process copious amounts of data quickly.
  - The internet and IT allow people to work from home or be self-employed.
- **Service industry:** accounts for **75% of the UK's economy**, including healthcare, IT support, and entertainment.
- **Finance and research:** jobs include accounting, insurance, and investment (e.g. Barclays, Aviva). Research is also essential for sustainable growth in the UK.
- **Science and business parks:** areas designed for company offices, often located near universities to attract graduates. For example, the UK has over **100 science parks**.

Impacts of industry on the environment
All specs except: CIE, Pearson IGCSE

- In the past, toxic waste polluted land and water supplies. **Coal mining** left ugly spoil heaps and transformed landscapes, and burning coal caused air pollution, such as the smog in London during the 1950s.
- While active coal mining has ceased in much of the UK, its environmental legacy persists. For example, Wales is home to approximately 40% of the UK's **coal tips** which pose risks of pollution, landslides, and spontaneous combustion, especially with increasing rainfall linked to climate change.
- A 2024 investigation revealed that 17 landfills across England are producing leachate containing **PFAS** or 'forever chemicals' at levels up to 260 times higher than deemed safe for drinking water. These substances are persistent in the environment and pose significant health risks.

Case study – past and present impacts

Torr Limestone Quarry, Somerset, UK	
Past environmental impacts:	**Present sustainable management practices:**
• Natural habitats destroyed. • Air pollution from emissions. • Landscapes were scarred by abandoned quarry sites.	• 80 hectares of land restored to grassland. • Regular monitoring of water quality, airborne emissions, and noise. • Chippings transported by rail to reduce road traffic and emissions.

The North-South Divide
All specs except: CIE, Pearson IGCSE

The **North-South Divide** refers to the **cultural and economic disparities** between the wealthier South of England and the less prosperous North. Strategies to address these regional differences include:
- **Relocation of professional jobs:** various companies are moving jobs to the North to boost the economy. For example, the **BBC** moved many of its offices to **Salford** in **2011**.
- **Devolution measures:** additional **power and funding** are given to councils in the North to improve local areas. For example, in **2014**, Manchester elected a mayor who was given £1 **billion** to improve the city and attract businesses. Further devolution deals, such as the **2023 Trailblazer agreement**, granted Greater Manchester additional powers over transport, housing, and regeneration, accompanied by a significant funding.

Socioeconomic changes in rural landscapes

All specs except: CIE, Pearson IGCSE

	South Cambridgeshire	Outer Hebrides
Population changes	• Population **increases** as more people (especially the **elderly**) move to the countryside for quality of life. • **25% of the population** are migrants, contributing to population growth.	• Population **decreases** as **young people** move away to find work. • **50% of the population** has left, leading to a decline in the local workforce.
Social impacts	• **Young people moving away:** high housing costs force young people to leave. • **Reduced public transport services:** increased car ownership reduces demand for public transport, leading to service cuts that affect non-car owners.	• **School closures:** fewer children may lead to schools shutting down. • **Ageing population:** an older population will require more **healthcare and social care**, increasing costs and pressure on services.
Economic impacts	• **Lack of affordable housing:** high demand affects prices for locals. • **Higher prices:** the costs of food, fuel, etc. experience increased demand. • **Pressure on social services**: increased population puts strain on services like **healthcare**.	• **Cost of services:** maintaining **ferries** and other essential services is expensive, and some **post offices** have closed. • **Tourism pressure:** tourism is popular, but the **infrastructure** is struggling to cope with demand.

Links between UK and the wider world

All specs except: CIE, Pearson IGCSE

- **Trade:** the UK is one of the world's largest economies and a major trading nation. It exports goods such as machinery, vehicles, pharmaceuticals, and financial services, while importing raw materials, food, and consumer goods. Since leaving the EU, the UK has negotiated trade agreements with countries like Japan, Australia, and New Zealand, and is seeking to expand its trade relationships globally.
- **Culture:** the UK is a global cultural powerhouse, exporting music, literature, film, and television. English is the most widely spoken second language globally, facilitating communication and cultural exchange.
- **Transport:** the UK is a major hub for international transport. Heathrow and Gatwick are among the busiest airports in the world, connecting the UK to hundreds of destinations. The Channel Tunnel links the UK to mainland Europe, providing transport route for goods and passengers.
- **Electronic communication:** The UK is a leader in electronic communication, with advanced internet and telecommunications networks. British media organizations like the BBC have a worldwide audience, spreading news, culture, and entertainment.
- **European Union (EU):** the UK officially left the EU in 2020, but it maintains economic and political ties through agreements like the Trade and Cooperation Agreement (TCA). The UK and EU continue to cooperate on issues like security, climate change, and research.
- **Commonwealth:** the Commonwealth is a political association of 56 member states, most of which were formerly part of the British Empire. It provides opportunities for trade and investment, with countries like India, Canada, and Australia being key partners. The Commonwealth promotes shared values like democracy, human rights, and sustainable development.

Improvements and new developments

All specs except: CIE, Pearson IGCSE

- **Road improvements:** a £2 billion project will add 1,600km of new lanes to motorways and major roads, improving links in southeast England. This will create jobs for construction workers and improve road networks, reducing congestion. However, it will also cause noise pollution and traffic during construction.
- **Railway improvements (HS2):** the HS2 is a high-speed train (232 mph) that will connect northern and southern England, reducing travel times. It cuts journey times in half and stimulates economic growth in northern England by improving access to higher-paying jobs in the south. However, it is extremely expensive and time-consuming to build and will damage the countryside. The HS2 was initially planned to extend to Manchester but this phase was cancelled and scaled back to only reach Birmingham due to rising costs and delays.
- **London Heathrow Expansion:** a new terminal at Heathrow Airport aims to ease congestion and allow for expansion. This increases passenger capacity, attracting more businesses and investors to the UK, but is highly expensive, costing £18.6 billion.

Resources affecting wellbeing

	Economic wellbeing	Social wellbeing
Food	• A well-fed population is more productive, leading to economic growth. • Malnutrition reduces workforce efficiency and increases healthcare costs.	• Access to sufficient, nutritious food improves health and life expectancy. • Food insecurity can lead to social unrest and inequality.
Water	• Essential for agriculture, industry, and energy production (e.g. hydroelectricity). • Lack of clean water limits economic development and increases costs for healthcare.	• Clean water is vital for health and hygiene, reducing diseases like cholera. • Water scarcity can lead to conflict and migration.
Energy	• Powers industries, transport, and technology, driving economic growth. • Reliable energy supply attracts investment and creates jobs.	• Access to electricity improves quality of life (e.g. lighting, heating, education). • Energy poverty traps people in poverty/inequality cycles.

Global inequalities in supply & consumption of resources

- **Food supply:** uneven due to climate, soil quality, and technology. LICs often face food shortages, while HICs experience food waste.
- **Food consumption:** HICs consume more calories and a wider variety of food options like organic produce. LICs rely on subsistence farming and have limited access to diverse diets.
- **Water supply:** uneven distribution due to climate, geography, and infrastructure. Water-rich areas (e.g. Amazon Basin) contrast with regions (e.g. Sub-Saharan Africa).
- **Water consumption:** HICs use more water per capita (e.g. for industry, agriculture, and domestic use). LICs often lack access to clean water, relying on unsafe sources.
- **Energy supply:** fossil fuels are unevenly distributed globally (e.g. oil in the Middle East). Renewable energy potential varies (e.g. solar in sunny regions, wind in coastal areas).
- **Energy consumption:** HICs like USA, China, and Russia consume far more energy per capita due to industrialisation and high living standards. LICs rely on traditional energy sources (e.g. wood, charcoal), which are less efficient and more polluting.

Resource use in the UK

All specs except: CIE, Pearson IGCSE

Food:
- **Growing demand for high-value food exports from LICs:** the UK imports exotic and high-value foods (e.g. coffee, spices, tropical fruits) from LICs. This benefits LIC economies but can lead to exploitation of workers.
- **All-year demand for seasonal and organic produce:** UK consumers expect seasonal foods (e.g. strawberries) to be available year-round, leading to imports from countries with different climates. Organic produce is increasingly popular due to health and environmental concerns.
- **Larger carbon footprints and food miles:** importing food from distant countries increases 'food miles' (distance food travels from farm to plate), contributing to carbon emissions. Growing movement towards local sourcing to reduce carbon footprints and support UK farmers.
- **Trend towards agribusiness:** involves large-scale, industrial farming to increase efficiency and output. It uses advanced technology and machinery but can harm the environment (e.g. loss of biodiversity, soil degradation).

Water:
- **Changing demand for water:** UK water demand is rising due to population growth, increased use of appliances (e.g. dishwashers), and higher living standards.
- **Water quality and pollution management:** pollution from agriculture (e.g. fertilizers, pesticides), industry, and sewage affects water quality. Strategies to manage pollution include legislation to limit pollutants, treatment plants to clean water, and education to reduce waste and pollution.
- **Matching supply and demand:** areas of surplus (i.e. north and west of the UK with high rainfall and low population density) vs. areas of deficit (i.e. south and east of the UK with low rainfall and high population density).
- **Water transfer:** to balance supply and demand, water is transferred from surplus areas (e.g. Wales) to deficit areas (e.g. London). This requires expensive infrastructure (e.g. pipelines, reservoirs) and can cause environmental and social issues.

Energy:
- **Changing energy mix:** the UK is shifting away from fossil fuels (coal, oil, gas) towards renewable energy (e.g. wind, solar, hydropower electricity). Renewables now account for a growing share of the UK's energy supply. However, the reliance on gas has increased as it is cheaper compared to oil.
- **Reduced domestic supplies of fossil fuels:** UK coal mines have closed due to depletion and environmental concerns. North Sea oil and gas reserves are declining, increasing reliance on imports.
- **Environmental issues:** fossil fuels cause air pollution and contribute to climate change. Renewable energy reduces emissions but can harm wildlife (e.g. wind turbines affecting migration of birds). Nuclear energy needs to be dealt with carefully, as leakage can cause serious environmental damage.

Global patterns of food supply

- **Calorie intake:** high in HICs due to wealth and access to diverse diets; low in LICs due to poverty, limited food availability, and malnourishment.
- **Food supply:** surplus in regions with advanced agriculture; deficit in regions with poor infrastructure, conflict, or harsh climates.
- **Reasons for increasing food consumption:** economic development: rising incomes allow people to afford more food and a greater variety (e.g. meat, dairy, processed foods). Urbanisation also increases demand for variety.
- **Rising population:** global population growth (expected to reach 9.7 billion by 2050) increases demand for food. Rapid growth in LICs and NEEs (Newly Emerging Economies) puts pressure on food supplies.

Factors affecting food supply

- **Climate:** extreme weather (e.g. droughts, floods) reduces crop yields. Climate change leads to unpredictable growing seasons and desertification.
- **Technology:** advanced technology (e.g. irrigation, GM crops) boosts food production in HICs, but LICs lack access to modern farming techniques.
- **Pests and disease:** crops and livestock are vulnerable to pests (e.g. locusts) and diseases; poor pest control in LICs reduces yields.
- **Water stress:** lack of water for irrigation limits food production, especially in arid (dry) regions. Overuse of water for agriculture depletes supplies and damages ecosystems.
- **Conflict:** wars disrupt farming, destroy infrastructure, and displace populations, leading to food shortages. Blockades and sanctions can prevent food imports.
- **Poverty:** poor farmers cannot afford seeds, machinery, or fertilisers to increase yields. Poverty limits access to food, even when it is available.

Impacts of food supply scarcity

- **Famine:** a severe shortage of food leads to widespread malnourishment, hunger, and death.
- **Undernutrition:** long-term lack of nutrients weakens immune systems, stunts growth, and reduces productivity.
- **Soil erosion:** over-farming and deforestation to grow more food degrade soil fertility, reducing future crop yields.
- **Rising prices:** food shortages increase prices, making food unaffordable for the poorest.
- **Social unrest:** food shortages and high prices can cause protests and riots.

Strategies to increase food supply

- **Irrigation:** artificially supplying water to crop roots to improve yield (e.g. drip irrigation for efficient water use, large-scale irrigation dams/canals).
  - Benefits: increases crop yields in dry areas.
  - Drawbacks: expensive initial costs.
- **Aeroponics and hydroponics:** growing plants in air using nutrient-rich water sprays (aeroponics) or in nutrient water instead of soil (hydroponics).
  - Benefits: efficient use of space, fast growth, and year-round production.
  - Drawbacks: high initial costs and reliance on technology.
- **The New Green Revolution:** focuses on improving yields in LICs through high-yield crop varieties (HYVs), better irrigation and fertilisers, and the use of GM (genetically modified) crops to resist pests and drought.
  - Benefits: increased food production and reduced hunger.
  - Drawbacks: environmental damage (e.g. soil degradation, water pollution) and inequality (small farmers may struggle to afford tech).
- **Biotechnology:** use of genetic engineering to create crops with desirable traits (e.g. pest resistance, drought tolerance).
  - Benefits: higher yields, reduced need for chemicals, and improved nutrition (e.g. Golden Rice with added Vitamin A).
  - Drawbacks: ethical concerns, potential environmental risks, and reliance on large corporations.
- **Appropriate technology:** simple, low-cost, and sustainable tools and techniques for LICs. Examples include treadle pumps for irrigation, and education on strategies like crop rotation or composting.
  - Benefits: affordable, easy to maintain, and environmentally friendly.
  - Drawbacks: require expertise and equipment that may not be available.

Case study – food supply projects

The Indus Basin Irrigation System, Pakistan	
Overview	• One of the largest irrigation systems in the world, supplying water to over 14 million hectares of farmland. • Uses a network of dams, canals, and reservoirs.
Advantages	• Increased food production (e.g. wheat, rice). • Increased use of hydroelectric power. • Improved incomes and reduced hunger.
Disadvantages	• Waterlogging damages soil. • People are deprived of water downstream.

SNAPREVISE

Sustainability strategies for food supply

- **Organic farming:** avoids synthetic chemicals such as pesticides and focuses on natural methods (e.g. crop rotation, composting). This protects biodiversity, reduces pollution, improves soil health.
- **Permaculture:** designing agricultural systems that mimic natural ecosystems. This focuses on sustainability, diversity, and minimal waste, while avoiding farming chemicals.
- **Urban and seasonal farming initiatives:** growing food in urban areas (e.g. rooftop gardens, vertical farming). Eating foods that are in season locally can also reduce imports and food miles to limit carbon emissions. This reduces food miles (distance food travels during importation or exportation), improves access to fresh produce, and uses urban spaces efficiently.
- **Fish and meat from sustainable sources:** sustainable fishing practices (e.g. quotas, fish farming) to prevent extinction of endangered fish species. For example, free-range and organic meat production is healthier and less harmful to animals and the environment.
- **Reduced waste and losses:** strategies include better storage, improved transport, and consumer education to reduce food waste. Around a third of the world's food is wasted, so this is a key target area for sustainable improvement. This means less waste and a more efficient food supply could enable redistribution of money and resources to address hunger, food poverty, and malnutrition.

Case study – food and water projects

The Makueni Food and Water Security Programme, Kenya	
Overview	A local scheme in Makueni County, Kenya, aimed at improving food and water security, including: • Rainwater harvesting tanks for irrigation. • Training farmers in sustainable farming techniques. • Growing drought-resistant crops.
Advantages	• Increased crop yields and food security. • Improved water availability for farming and households. • Low-cost and sustainable methods.
Disadvantages	• Limited funding and resources can restrict the scope. • Success depends on community participation and long-term maintenance.

Global patterns of water supply

All specs except: *CIE*

Water supply is uneven across the globe, with some regions (like tropical and temperate zones) receiving abundant rainfall, while others (like deserts) face severe scarcity.

- **Water surplus:** areas with high rainfall and low population density (e.g. Canada, Brazil, Russia), have abundant freshwater resources.
- **Water deficit:** areas with low rainfall and high population density (e.g. North Africa, the Middle East, parts of South Asia). These regions experience water scarcity due to arid climates and overuse.
- **Increasing water consumption:** this is largely due to two factors:
  - **Economic development:** industrial growth increases water demand for manufacturing and energy production. Rising living standards lead to higher domestic water use (e.g. showers, washing machines). Agriculture in developing economies requires more water for irrigation.
  - **Rising population:** global population growth increases demand for drinking water, sanitation, and food production. Urbanisation concentrates water demand in cities, often exceeding the supply.

Factors affecting water supply

All specs except: *CIE*

- **Climate:** areas with low rainfall or seasonal rainfall (e.g. deserts, monsoon regions) face water shortages. Climate change worsens droughts and reduces water availability in some regions.
- **Geology:** permeable rocks (e.g. sandstone) allow water to infiltrate and form aquifers, providing underground water supplies. Areas with impermeable rocks (e.g. granite) may lack groundwater resources.
- **Pollution of supply:** refers to industrial waste, agricultural runoff (e.g. fertilizers, pesticides), and untreated sewage contaminating water sources. Polluted water is unsafe for agriculture, industry, and especially drinking.
- **Overabstraction:** refers to excessive removal of water from rivers, lakes, and aquifers depletes supplies. This can lead to drying up of rivers.
- **Limited infrastructure:** poor infrastructure in LICs/NEEs limits access to clean water (e.g. lack of pipes, reservoirs, or treatment plants).
- **Poverty:** poor communities cannot afford water infrastructure or access to clean water. Reliance on unsafe water sources or the need to travel far distances for water increases health risks.

Impacts of water supply scarcity

All specs except: CIE

- **Waterborne disease and water pollution:** contaminated water spreads diseases like cholera. Poor sanitation and polluted water sources increase health risks, especially in LICs.
- **Food production:** lack of water for irrigation reduces crop yields, leading to food shortages and higher prices. Droughts can devastate agriculture, especially in arid regions.
- **Industrial output:** industries reliant on water (e.g. textiles, energy production) may reduce output or shut down during water shortages. This impacts economic growth and employment.
- **Potential for conflict:** water scarcity can lead to disputes between countries or regions sharing water sources (e.g. River Nile, River Ganges). Competition for water resources may escalate into political or military conflict where demand exceeds supply.

Strategies to increase water supply

All specs except: CIE

- **Diverting supplies and increasing storage:** diverting rivers or streams to areas of need and storing water in reservoirs or underground aquifers.
  - Benefits: reduces water loss and provides reliable supply in dry periods.
  - Drawbacks: can be expensive and difficult to coordinate, may necessitate diverting water to storage for long-term benefit even if there is short-term urgent need.
- **Dams and reservoirs:** dams block rivers to create reservoirs, storing water for domestic, agricultural, and industrial use. For example, Kielder Dam in Northumberland is the largest reservoir in the UK.
  - Benefits: provides a reliable water supply, generates hydroelectric power, and controls flooding.
  - Drawbacks: expensive, can displace communities and harm ecosystems.
- **Water transfers:** moving water from areas of surplus to areas of deficit via pipelines, canals, or aqueducts.
  - Benefits: balances water supply and demand across regions.
  - Drawbacks: expensive, can cause environmental damage, and may lead to political tensions if needing to transfer water from one area in need to another more urgent one.
- **Desalination:** removing salt from seawater to make it drinkable (e.g. Ras Al Khair in Saudi Arabia is the world's largest desalination plant).
  - Benefits: provides a reliable water source in dry regions.
  - Drawbacks: high energy use, expensive, and produces brine waste that can harm marine ecosystems.

Case study – water development projects

All specs except: CIE

The South–North Water Transfer Project, China	
Key details	• Transfers water from the water-rich south (Yangtze River) to the drier north (Beijing, Tianjin). • Includes three routes: Eastern, Central, and Western.
Benefits	• Provides water to cities and industries in northern China, supporting economic growth. • Reduces water shortages in areas of deficit.
Costs	• Expensive: estimated cost of over USD\$70 billion. • Displacement of people: over 300,000 people relocated. • Environmental impacts: habitat loss and reduced water flow.

Sustainability strategies for water supply

All specs except: CIE

- **Water conservation:** reducing water waste through efficient use and better management (e.g. fixing leaks, water-efficient appliances).
- **Groundwater management:** monitoring and controlling underground water sources to prevent overabstraction (e.g. regulation, recharging aquifers).
- **Recycling:** treating wastewater to be reused for agriculture, industry, or domestic purposes (e.g. Singapore's "NEWater" recycles wastewater).
- **'Grey' water:** reusing water from sinks, baths, and washing machines for non-drinking purposes (e.g. irrigation, flushing toilets).

Case study – sustainable water supply

All specs except: CIE

The Wakel River Basin Project, India	
Key details	• Located in Rajasthan, India, an arid region with water scarcity. • Aims to improve water supply through sustainable methods including: **taankas** (underground storage systems to collect rainwater and prevent evaporation), **johed** (small earth dams to capture rainwater and recharge groundwater) and **pats** (irrigation channels to distribute water efficiently).
Benefits	• Increased water availability for drinking and farming. • Improved crop yields and reduced poverty. • Low-cost and sustainable, using local materials.
Costs	• Limited to small-scale use; cannot service large populations. • Success depends on community participation/maintenance.

Energy supply

Global patterns of energy supply

- **High consumption:** in HICs like the UK, USA, and Australia due to industrialisation, high living standards, and reliance on energy-intensive technologies.
- **Low consumption:** in LICs like Somalia, Gambia, and Haiti due to limited access to energy infrastructure and lower demand.
- **Energy surplus:** in energy-rich regions (e.g. Middle East for oil, Russia for gas, China for coal).
- **Energy deficit:** in energy-poor regions (e.g. Sub-Saharan Africa, parts of South Asia) due to lack of resources or infrastructure.
- **Increasing energy consumption:** this is largely due to three factors:
  - **Economic development:** industrial growth in NEEs (Newly Emerging Economies) like China and India increases energy demand for manufacturing and transport. Rising incomes lead to higher energy use for domestic appliances, heating, and cooling.
  - **Rising population:** global population growth increases demand for energy for housing, transport, and food production. Urbanisation concentrates energy demand in cities.
  - **Technology:** advances in technology increase energy use (e.g. widespread use of smartphones, electric vehicles, and data centres). However, energy-efficient technologies (e.g. LED lighting, renewable energy systems) can reduce per capita energy consumption in some areas.

Factors affecting energy supply

- **Physical factors:** availability of natural resources (e.g. oil, gas, coal, sunlight, wind). Fossil fuels are found in specific locations, and renewable energy potential depends on climate and geography.
- **Cost of exploitation and production:** extracting fossil fuels or building renewable energy infrastructure can be expensive. LICs may lack the financial resources to exploit their energy reserves.
- **Technology:** advanced technology is needed to extract energy from difficult locations (e.g. deep-sea oil drilling, fracking). LICs may lack access to such technology, limiting their energy supply.
- **Political factors:** political instability in energy-rich regions (e.g. Middle East, Russia) can disrupt supply. Trade disputes, sanctions, and conflicts can limit energy exports. Countries may prioritise energy security by reducing reliance on imports (e.g. UK investing in renewables).

Impacts of energy supply scarcity

- **Exploration of environmentally sensitive areas:** energy insecurity drives exploration in remote or sensitive areas (e.g. Arctic oil drilling, Amazon rainforest). This results in environmental damage (e.g. oil spills, deforestation) and comes with many risks to local communities and the global climate.
- **Economic and environmental costs:** energy shortages increase prices, affecting industries and households. Over-reliance on fossil fuels leads to air pollution and climate change.
- **Food production:** energy is required for irrigation, machinery, and transport in agriculture. Energy shortages can reduce food production, leading to higher prices and food insecurity.
- **Industrial output:** industries reliant on energy (e.g. manufacturing, mining) may reduce output or shut down during shortages. This impacts economic growth and employment.
- **Potential for conflict:** competition for energy resources can lead to disputes between countries or regions. Energy insecurity can exacerbate existing political tensions.

Case study – energy supply projects

Shale gas extraction (fracking), USA	
Key details	• Fracking involves injecting water, sand, and chemicals into shale rock to release natural gas • Fracking occurs in more than 30 states in the USA
Benefits	• Increases domestic energy supply, reducing reliance on imports and creating jobs to boost the economy • Natural gas is cleaner than coal and oil
Costs	• Risk of groundwater contamination from chemicals • Causes minor earthquakes • High water usage and environmental damage • Releases methane which is a highly toxic and potent greenhouse gas • Poorly regulated in the USA making it hard to monitor pollution and violation of safety rules • Banned in other countries like the UK due to its environmental impact